D0438297

Property Rights

Other Books in the Bill of Rights series:

The Bill of Rights

| Property Rights

Kimberly Troisi-Paton, Book Editor

GREENHAVEN PRESS

An imprint of Thomson Gale, a part of The Thomson Corporation

THOMSON

™

GALE

Detroit • New York • San Francisco • New Haven, Conn. • Waterville, Maine • London

Christine Nasso, *Publisher*
Elizabeth Des Chenes, *Managing Editor*

© 2007 Thomson Gale, a part of The Thomson Corporation.

Thomson and Star logo are trademarks and Gale and Greenhaven Press are registered trademarks used herein under license.

For more information, contact:
Greenhaven Press
27500 Drake Rd.
Farmington Hills, MI 48331-3535
Or you can visit our Internet site at http://www.gale.com

ALL RIGHTS RESERVED
No part of this work covered by the copyright hereon may be reproduced or used in any form or by any means—graphic, electronic, or mechanical, including photocopying, record-ing, taping, Web distribution, or information storage retrieval systems—without the written permission of the publisher.

Articles in Greenhaven Press anthologies are often edited for length to meet page require-ments. In addition, original titles of these works are changed to clearly present the main thesis and to explicitly indicate the author's opinion. Every effort is made to ensure that Greenhaven Press accurately reflects the original intent of the authors. Every effort has been made to trace the owners of copyrighted material.

Cover photograph reproduced by permission of AP/Wide World Photos.

LIBRARY OF CONGRESS CATALOGING-IN-PUBLICATION DATA

Property rights / Kimberly Troisi-Paton, book editor.
  p. cm. -- (Bill of Rights)
Includes bibliographical references and index.
ISBN-13: 978-0-7377-3543-7 (lib. : alk. paper)
ISBN-10: 0-7377-3543-0 (lib. : alk. paper)
1. Right of property--United States. 2. Eminent domain--United States. I. Troisi-Paton, Kimberly.
  KF562.P758 2007
  346.7304--dc22
                                                          2006022970

Printed in the United States of America
10 9 8 7 6 5 4 3 2 1

Contents

Chapter 3: The Supreme Court and Regulatory Takings

In *Nollan v. California Coastal Commission* (1987), the Court found that requiring property owners to permit public use of their private property went beyond mere land-use regulation and constituted a taking as defined by the Fifth Amendment.

Chapter 4: Current Issues and Perspectives on Property Rights

A syndicated columnist contends that state and local governments are using eminent domain to steal property from ordinary citizens in order to enrich developers and increase the tax base.

"I cannot agree with those who think of the Bill of Rights as an 18th century straitjacket, unsuited for this age. . . . The evils it guards against are not only old, they are with us now, they exist today."

Hugo Black, associate justice of the U.S. Supreme Court, 1937–1971

Foreword

The Bill of Rights codifies the freedoms most essential to American democracy. Freedom of speech, freedom of religion, the right to bear arms, the right to a trial by a jury of one's peers, the right to be free from cruel and unusual punishment—these are just a few of the liberties that the Founding Fathers thought it necessary to spell out in the first ten amendments to the U.S. Constitution.

While the document itself is quite short (consisting of fewer than five hundred words), and while the liberties it protects often seem straightforward, the Bill of Rights has been a source of debate ever since its creation. Throughout American history, the rights the document protects have been tested and reinterpreted. Again and again, individuals perceiving violations of their rights have sought redress in the courts. The courts in turn have struggled to decipher the original intent of the founders as well as the need to accommodate changing societal norms and values.

The ultimate responsibility for addressing these claims has fallen to the U.S. Supreme Court. As the highest court in the nation, it is the Supreme Court's role to interpret the Constitution. The Court has considered numerous cases in which people have accused government of impinging on their rights.

In the process, the Court has established a body of case law and precedents that have, in a sense, defined the Bill of Rights. In doing so, the Court has often reversed itself and introduced new ideas and approaches that have altered the legal meaning of the rights contained in the Bill of Rights. As a general rule, the Court has erred on the side of caution, upholding and expanding the rights of individuals rather than restricting them.

An example of this trend is the definition of cruel and unusual punishment. The Eighth Amendment specifically states, "Excessive bail shall not be required, nor excessive fines imposed, nor cruel and unusual punishments inflicted." However, over the years the Court has had to grapple with defining what constitutes "cruel and unusual punishment." In colonial America, punishments for crimes included branding, the lopping off of ears, and whipping. Indeed, these punishments were considered lawful at the time the Bill of Rights was written. Obviously, none of these punishments are legal today. In order to justify outlawing certain types of punishment that are deemed repugnant by the majority of citizens, the Court has ruled that it must consider the prevailing opinion of the masses when making such decisions. In overturning the punishment of a man stripped of his citizenship, the Court stated in 1958 that it must rely on society's "evolving standards of decency" when determining what constitutes cruel and unusual punishment. Thus the definition of cruel and unusual is not frozen to include only the types of punishment that were illegal at the time of the framing of the Bill of Rights; specific modes of punishment can be rejected as society deems them unjust.

Another way that the Courts have interpreted the Bill of Rights to expand individual liberties is through the process of "incorporation." Prior to the passage of the Fourteenth Amendment, the Bill of Rights was thought to prevent only the federal government from infringing on the rights listed in the document. However, the Fourteenth Amendment, which was passed in the wake of the Civil War, includes the words, "... nor shall any state deprive any person of life, liberty, or property, without due process of law; nor deny to any person within its jurisdiction the equal protection of the laws." Citing this passage, the Court has ruled that many of the liberties contained in the Bill of Rights apply to state and local governments as well as the federal government. This process of incorporation laid the legal foundation for the civil rights movement—most specifically the 1954 *Brown v. Board of Education* ruling that put an end to legalized segregation.

As these examples reveal, the Bill of Rights is not static. It truly is a living document that is constantly being reinterpreted and redefined. The Bill of Rights series captures this vital aspect of one of America's most cherished founding texts. Each volume in the series focuses on one particular right protected in the Bill of Rights. Through the use of primary and secondary sources, the right's evolution is traced from colonial times to the present. Primary sources include landmark Supreme Court rulings, speeches by prominent experts, and editorials. Secondary sources include historical analyses, law journal articles, book excerpts, and magazine articles. Each book also includes several features to facilitate research, including a bibliography, an annotated table of contents, an annotated list of relevant Supreme Court cases, an introduction, and an index. These elements help to make the Bill of Rights series a fascinating and useful tool for examining the fundamental liberties of American democracy.

Greenhaven Press anthologies primarily consist of previously published material taken from a variety of sources, including periodicals, books, scholarly journals, newspapers, government documents, and position papers from private and public organizations. These original sources are often edited for length and to ensure their accessibility for a young adult audience. The anthology editors also add subheads and change the original titles of these works in order to clearly present the main thesis of each viewpoint and to explicitly indicate the opinion presented in the viewpoint. These alterations are made in consideration of both the reading and comprehension levels of a young adult audience. Every effort is made to ensure that Greenhaven Press accurately reflects the original intent of the authors included in this anthology.

Introduction

"Nor shall private property be taken for public use without just compensation." It is a simple phrase, a final sentence fragment tacked onto the very end of the Fifth Amendment. Of the Fifth Amendment's several components, all of which seem to generate great debate at the U.S. Supreme Court, none has led to more perplexing case law than the takings clause. In the history of Supreme Court jurisprudence, these dozen words have sparked nearly unparalleled controversy. They have pitted private property owners against nearly every permutation of government authority in the United States—local municipalities, cities, states, development corporations, and planning agencies. The words have also pitted judge against judge, creating an area of the law full of scathing dissents and narrowly decided Supreme Court rulings.

Per Se Takings

Simply put, the Fifth Amendment is intended to prevent the government from taking people's private property without compensating them for it. There are generally two types of "takings": per se takings and regulatory takings. Per se takings are fairly straightforward. The government takes ownership of the land outright, usually for a commonly accepted public purpose such as to build a highway or construct a municipal building. The process through which the government takes the property is known as eminent domain. As long as the owner is provided just compensation for the property, the taking is considered constitutional.

Although the eminent domain procedure is a generally accepted practice, property owners have challenged per se takings in court. They have sued on the grounds that the compensation for their property was not just, that the process for determining and awarding the compensation was unfair, and that their property was not being seized for a legitimate public use. These challenges highlight the complexity of the issues. There are many different ways to appraise and value property and many ways to award money to people under the law—through a jury, through a judge, or through a legislative predetermination. There also are many different opinions with respect to what is an acceptable public use. For example, in the controversial *Kelo v. City of New London* case (2005), the Supreme Court permitted aging residences to be acquired and destroyed to make way for a city development project. The ousted homeowners did not think that a proposal for urban redevelopment was an appropriate public use; the city, along with the Supreme Court, obviously did not agree.

Regulatory Takings

Regulatory takings cases are even less simple to resolve. A regulatory taking occurs when government regulations, such as zoning restrictions and environmental policies, limit the ways property can be used by its owner, thereby diminishing the property's value. The courts have been forced to grapple with how to define a regulatory taking. Specifically, they must determine at what point the government's regulation of private property becomes so economically burdensome to the owner that financial compensation is required; that is, when does a mere regulation become an actual taking.

One of the early precedents for regulatory takings law was *Pennsylvania Coal Company v. Mahon* (1922). In that case, the Supreme Court examined a Pennsylvania law that prevented coal companies from mining underground if the mining would cause a house on the surface of the land to collapse. The Court found that if the homeowners had only purchased surface property rights, the coal companies could not be prohibited from mining below the surface. Justice Oliver Wendell Holmes famously expressed the fact that a taking might occur if a loss in property value occurs—even without a physical appropriation of the property. "What makes the right to mine coal valuable is that it can be exercised with profit. To make it commercially impracticable to mine certain coal has very nearly the same effect for constitutional purposes as appropriating or destroying it." Thus, according to the Court, the regulation on mining went too far even though no property was actually seized by the government.

In 1978 the Court heard what many scholars consider to be the first of the regulatory takings cases, *Penn Central Transportation Company v. City of New York*. The case involved a conflict over New York City's Grand Central Station. The railroad company wanted to develop the property, but the city had designated it a historic landmark, requiring approval from the city's Landmarks Preservation Commission to make alterations. The Court ruled that the regulation on the development of the property did not amount to a taking. In his majority opinion in the case, Justice William Brennan crafted a balancing test. Essentially, the Court had to determine on a case-by-case basis when the government's actions exceeded mere regulation and constituted a taking. So long as the owner retained a reasonable use of the property, and so long as the regulation was reasonably related to a legitimate government interest, then no regulatory taking had occurred. According to Brennan, a balancing approach to regulatory takings was necessary because so far the Court had been unable to establish clear guidelines that could apply to all cases.

Applying the Balancing Test

Since *Penn Central*, property owners have challenged numerous government regulations on the grounds that they have amounted to takings. In most cases the Supreme Court has refused to find in favor of property owners. According to various Supreme Court cases, governmental authorities can manage marshes and wetlands, designate historic landmarks, zone forest preserves, and temporarily call a halt to development.

Basically, anything less than a complete deprivation of property use will not be deemed a regulatory taking. The Court has, at times, attempted to phrase the test in a black-and-white formula; yet, a regulatory takings analysis always seems to boil down to the same basic *Penn Central* balance.

However, the Court has found in favor of property owners in some cases. In one significant case, *Lucas v. South Carolina Coastal Council* (1992), a developer brought a case in South Carolina when all further beachfront development was prohibited on a barrier island. The Supreme Court decided that the developer, who could no longer build, was deprived of all beneficial use of his land. Accordingly, a regulatory taking had occurred, and the developer was entitled to compensation.

Other cases in which regulation has been deemed to have gone too far have been termed *exactions* cases. These cases involve government authorities asking property owners for use of their property in exchange for something that the property owner wants. For example, in *Dolan v. City of Tigard* (1994), city authorities wanted to provide the public with a bike and pedestrian path. Whenever a business with property bordering the path sought to expand, the city would grant a building permit only if the business allowed the public to use part of the property as a path. The city would not monetarily compensate the business for the public use of part of the property but would grant the permit. The Supreme Court determined that such an exaction was a taking.

The *Dolan* case helps to illustrate the logic of regulatory takings. The exaction is not a per se taking because a private business still owns the land. However, the business no longer has any control over how a certain part of the land is used. By taking control of the property, the government effectively drains it of all financial worth. Therefore, the regulation functions as if the government had seized the property outright. As Justice Oliver Wendell Holmes noted long ago in the *Penn-*

sylvania Coal case, the result of taking control over property is really the same as simply taking ownership of the property away.

Takings in the Twenty-first Century

As a result of the difficulties inherent in defining takings, the case law on regulatory takings is far from clear. Yet in one sense, it is comforting to know that something as important as property rights will be determined in accordance with the particular circumstances of any given case. After all, property rights do differ from one case to another and even from one time to another.

For instance, in the twentieth century judges considered matters such as the installation of broadcast antennae on the roofs of homes and apartment buildings. Now, at only the beginning of the twenty-first century, judges must consider technological advances such as digital cable broadcast streams. Digital streams do not physically touch anything, but they involve significant property rights and render the broadcast antennae obsolete. Under such circumstances, the law clearly benefits from being able to change with the circumstances of each particular case. Thus, there is no doubt that takings law will remain controversial and admittedly problematic to even the greatest of minds.

The History of the Protection from Unfair Seizure of Property

The History of the Power of Eminent Domain

Donald W. Detisch

In the following excerpt from an article published in San Diego Lawyer *magazine, attorney Donald W. Detisch summarizes the history of the power of eminent domain. This power of the government to seize land, provided that compensation is made, may have originated in biblical times. Eventually the power of eminent domain appeared in England's Magna Carta and was later included in the Fifth Amendment to the U.S. Constitution.*

Donald W. Detisch chairs the Eminent Domain Section of the San Diego County Bar Association. His law practice includes condemnation and land-use law.

Eminent domain (*Dominium eminens*) is the power of the sovereign to take property for public use without the owner's consent upon making just compensation (*United States v. Jones* 109 U.S. 513; *Gilmer v. Lime Point*, 18 Cal. 229). The power of eminent domain is not a property right or an exercise by the state of ultimate ownership in the soil, but it is a power based on the sovereignty of the state. The origin of the power of eminent domain is indeed murky and was believed to have started during biblical times when King Ahab, urged by Jezebel, acquired Naboth's vineyard with Naboth being stoned to death for refusing to sell his land. (Fortunately, this practice was not continued to the present.)

With the demise of the Roman Empire, eminent domain disappeared for centuries, and during the medieval period when the demand for public improvements was small and the rights of individuals little regarded, eminent domain was neither considered nor discussed. The medieval feudal system de-

Donald W. Detisch, "Private vs. Public," *San Diego Lawyer*, January–February, 2006. Reproduced by permission.

clined and the concepts of individual ownership and the rights of private property rose, causing the eminent domain power to be recognized.

England's Magna Carta

In England, common law recognized the king's right to enter private property to erect defenses against public enemies or the ravages of the sea. The king's right to seize provisions for the royal household's use for compensation was regulated by the Magna Carta. Eminent domain grew out of the ancient proceeding known as Inquest of Office. This was an inquiry from jurors concerning any matter that entitled the king to the possession of lands, tenements, goods and chattels, and it was originally invoked in the case of escheat or forfeiture.

America's Adoption of Eminent Domain

The power of eminent domain was thus well established in England by the time of the American Revolution, and the obligation to pay compensation had become a necessary incident to the exercise of the power. The founders of our Constitution shared [English Philosopher John] Locke's affection for private property. In its conception, America adopted English land use law: "The supreme power cannot take from any man any part of his property without his own consent; for the preservation of property being the end of government and that for which men enter into society, it necessarily supposes and requires that the people should have property, without which they must be supposed to lose that, by entering into society, which was the end for which they entered into it." [Locke, *Second Treatise of Civil Government*]

During colonial times, eminent domain was justified only if the land were to be reserved for public use, which in most early cases involved the building of roads. The constitutions of Pennsylvania and Virginia were the first to use the phrase "public use," which was later included in the Fifth Amendment to the Constitution (afterward included in the 14th Amendment): "No person . . . shall be deprived of life, liberty, or property without the due process of law; nor shall private property be taken for public use, without just compensation."

SAN JUAN ISLAND LIBRARY
1010 GUARD STREET
FRIDAY HARBOR, WA 98250

An Essay on Property Rights

James Madison

James Madison is commonly referred to as the father of the U.S. Constitution. He drafted much of that document and most of the Bill of Rights, including the Fifth Amendment, which contains the takings clause. He held public offices in Virginia during the Revolutionary War era and later served as the fourth president of the United States.

In the following piece, which was published in the National Gazette *in 1792, Madison expresses his theory of the meaning of property. He defines property broadly to include material goods and personal opinions. He argues that the government must compensate individuals if it takes away any type of property—either directly or indirectly.*

This term ["property"] in its particular application means "that dominion which one man claims and exercises over the external things of the world, in exclusion of every other individual."

In its larger and juster meaning, it embraces every thing to which a man may attach a value and have a right; and *which leaves to every one else the like advantage.*

In the former sense, a man's land, or merchandize, or money is called his property.

In the latter sense, a man has a property in his opinions and the free communication of them.

He has a property of peculiar value in his religious opinions, and in the profession and practice dictated by them.

He has a property very dear to him in the safety and liberty of his person.

He has an equal property in the free use of his faculties and free choice of the objects on which to employ them.

James Madison, "Property," in *National Gazette*, March 29, 1792.

In a word, as a man is said to have a right to his property, he may be equally said to have a property in his rights.

Where an excess of power prevails, property of no sort is duly respected. No man is safe in his opinions, his person, his faculties, or his possessions.

Where there is an excess of liberty, the effect is the same, tho' from an opposite cause.

The Role of Government

Government is instituted to protect property of every sort; as well that which lies in the various rights of individuals, as that which the term particularly expresses. This being the end of government, that alone is a *just* government, which *impartially* secures to every man, whatever is his *own*.

According to this standard of merit, the praise of affording a just securing to property, should be sparingly bestowed on a government which, however scrupulously guarding the possessions of individuals, does not protect them in the enjoyment and communication of their opinions, in which they have an equal, and in the estimation of some, a more valuable property.

More sparingly should this praise be allowed to a government, where a man's religious rights are violated by penalties, or fettered by tests, or taxed by a hierarchy. Conscience is the most sacred of all property; other property depending in part on positive law, the exercise of that, being a natural and unalienable right. To guard a man's house as his castle, to pay public and enforce private debts with the most exact faith, can give no title to invade a man's conscience which is more sacred than his castle, or to withhold from it that debt of protection, for which the public faith is pledged, by the very nature and original conditions of the social pact.

That is not a just government, nor is property secure under it, where the property which a man has in his personal safety and personal liberty, is violated by arbitrary seizures of one class of citizens for the service of the rest. . . .

That is not a just government, nor is property secure under it, where arbitrary restrictions, exemptions, and monopolies deny to part of its citizens that free use of their faculties, and free choice of their occupations, which not only constitute their property in the general sense of the word; but are the means of acquiring property strictly so called. What must be the spirit of legislation where a manufacturer of linen cloth is forbidden to bury his own child in a linen shroud, in order to favour his neighbour who manufactures woolen cloth; where the manufacturer and wearer of woolen cloth are again forbidden the economical use of buttons of that material, in favor of the manufacturer of buttons of other materials!

A just security to property is not afforded by that government, under which unequal taxes oppress one species of property and reward another species: where arbitrary taxes invade the domestic sanctuaries of the rich, and excessive taxes grind the faces of the poor; where the keenness and competitions of want are deemed an insufficient spur to labor, and taxes are again applied, by an unfeeling policy, as another spur; in violation of that sacred property, which Heaven, in decreeing man to earn his bread by the sweat of his brow, kindly reserved to him, in the small repose that could be spared from the supply of his necessities.

The Government Must Compensate For Taking Any Property

If there be a government then which prides itself in maintaining the inviolability of property; which provides that none shall be taken *directly* even for public use without indemnification to the owner, and yet *directly* violates the property which individuals have in their opinions, their religion, their persons, and their faculties; nay more, which *indirectly* violates their property, in their actual possessions, in the labor that acquires their daily subsistence, and in the hallowed remnant of time which ought to relieve their fatigues and soothe their cares, the influence will have been anticipated, that such a government is not a pattern for the United States.

If the United States mean to obtain or deserve the full praise due to wise and just governments, they will equally respect the rights of property, and the property in rights: they will rival the government that most sacredly guards the former; and by repelling its example in violating the latter, will make themselves a pattern to that and all other governments.

The Meaning of the Takings Clause

Jay M. Feinman

In the following excerpt law professor Jay M. Feinman presents his view of the founding fathers' original intent in writing the takings clause of the Fifth Amendment. Feinman rejects the arguments of conservatives who contend that the clause was meant to require government to compensate individuals for any government use or regulation of their property. Instead, Feinman maintains, the founders had a more liberal view of property as existing for the common good and the general use of society. Therefore, he concludes, the takings clause was meant to have a more limited application: Compensation was only required if a person's property was physically taken away from him.

Jay M. Feinman is a professor at Rutgers School of Law. He has authored several articles and books about the common law, including Un-Making Law: The Conservative Campaign to Roll Back the Common Law.

Because conservatives usually emphasize the need for strict construction of the Constitution and adherence to the original understanding of the framers, the story begins, as most stories about American law begin, at the time of the founding. According to property rights advocates, the colonists, the framers of the Constitution and the Bill of Rights, and the leaders of the early republic had a vision of government and property that was "liberal" in the classical sense and that led them to enact a constitutional limitation on the regulation of property. Liberalism rested on two fundamental tenets: First, rights are individual and prepolitical, held by people

Jay M. Feinman, *Un-Making Law: The Conservative Campaign to Roll Back Common Law*. Boston: Beacon Press, 2004, pp. 164–68. Copyright © 2004 by Jay M. Feinman. All rights reserved. Reproduced by permission of Beacon Press, Boston.

by the law of nature and not by the will of the state. Second, the function of government is to protect those natural rights. (Beginning in the late nineteenth century, liberal individualism would take a less-religious, more materialistic form, particularly among economists, who emphasized the power of grasping self-interest as the prime mover and greatest good of society.)

Locke's Influence on the Takings Clause

The patron saint of liberalism for property rights advocates is the political philosopher John Locke. As seen by conservatives, Locke believed that all people are "naturally in ... a state of perfect freedom to order their actions, and dispose of their possessions, and persons as they think fit, within the bounds of the law of nature, without asking leave, or depending upon the will of any other man." In exercising that freedom, people acquire property, not through the grant of government but through their own appropriation of the world of nature. "God, when he gave the world in common to all mankind, commanded man also to labour. . . . He that in obedience to this command of God, subdued, tilled and sowed any part of it, thereby annexed to it something that was his property, which had no title to, nor could without injury take from him."

The conservative account caricatures Locke. The deeply religious Locke would have rejected the later liberal view that property is merely a means for looking out for Number One. Property was a gift from God to be used and not wasted and to benefit all humanity, not just those who can grab the most of it. Locke explained in words that would place him in the left wing of today's Democratic Party: "But though this be a state of liberty, yet it is not a state of license." The fruits of labor become property, "at least where there is enough and as good left in common for others." Moreover, "charity gives every man a title to so much out of another's Plenty, as will keep him from extream [sic] want, where he has no means to

27

subsist otherwise." (Religious values still count in the property rights debate. The national Conference of Catholic Bishops, the United Methodist Church's General Board of Church and Society, and the Religious Action Center of Reform Judaism all have opposed takings legislation; the Methodist Social Principles, for example, state "We believe private ownership is a trusteeship under God . . . but is limited by the overriding needs of society.")

Locke's religiosity and expression of the limits of property undermine the view of him as an advocate of unfettered, absolute private property rights, so they are often ignored or discarded by conservatives. [Professor Richard] Epstein, for example, presumes to correct Locke, by dispensing with the idea of divine justification for private property, a correction akin, as law professor Thomas Ross noted, to claiming that Christianity is consistent with Judaism, with a modest correction recognizing Jesus Christ as the Son of God.

The Founding Fathers and Colonial Views

The problem runs much deeper than misreading a particular writer. The political philosophy known as "republicanism" was at least coequal with liberalism and probably dominant in the founding era. Republicans viewed rights as constructed by the state, not as natural artifacts, and constructed for a particular purpose: to advance the common good. Property, therefore, is not a natural right, nor should it serve the selfish interests of individuals. Property is created, defined, and limited by law to promote the general welfare. The most noted republican in theory and action, Thomas Jefferson, pushed measures in Virginia to revamp the inheritance and landholding laws to reduce dynastic wealth and to allow emigrants to the undeveloped western territories to acquire land, principles that subsequently were adopted for the Northwest Territories and the lands of the Louisiana Purchase. "Legislators cannot invent too many devices for subdividing land," he wrote, making clear that property was a social construct the purpose of which was collective, not individual benefit.

The diverse attitudes toward property at the time of the founding are reflected in the law of eminent domain and the history of the takings clause. Two essential points undercut conservative mythmaking about the long-standing, fundamental nature of property rights. First, from colonial times through the drafting of the Fifth Amendment's takings clause and for decades after, the law did not generally prohibit government from taking property without paying for it. Second, "taking" meant then what it means today—to take, not to regulate—so there was no requirement of compensation when government action diminished property rights short of physically taking away the subject of the property.

In English law, the supremacy of Parliament enabled it to decide whether and how it would compensate owners for property taken. This power was carried over to the colonial legislatures. Only two of the colonial charters—Massachusetts and Carolina, the latter drafted by John Locke but never fully implemented—provided for compensation, and Massachusetts's provision was limited to goods, not land. None of the state constitutions enacted in 1776 included a compensation requirement, and by 1820 a majority still did not include such a provision. Even though states were not constitutionally obligated to do so, they did often provide some compensation when land was taken for road building or to be given to entrepreneurs for the construction of canals or other improvements. Often but not always: Several states did not compensate the owners because they presumed that the original grant from the colonial proprietors to the owners included an excess amount of property to account for any that should be taken by the government in the future. And the amount of compensation was up to the legislature or executive officials and was not reviewed by the courts; if the compensation was given in land unrelated to the cash value of the loss, or if the compensation for an industrial site was based only on its value as uncultivated agricultural land, so be it.

"Takings" Did Not Include Regulation

In addition, any requirement of compensation could not have applied when property was regulated, because government regulation of property was ubiquitous. Another great conservative myth is that big government was a creation of Franklin Roosevelt, that prior to the New Deal the economy hummed along without interference. (Thus the Reaganite metaphor of "lifting government off our backs," to restore us to a pristine past of rugged individuals unfettered by the state.) In fact, government regulation of economy, morality, and everyday life was pervasive for decades before and after the framing of the Constitution. Land use was tightly controlled. From its founding, for example, Virginia limited the amount of tobacco landowners could plant and required them to grow other crops. During and after the Revolution, legislatures obliterated the property interests of British citizens and American loyalists. Virginia allowed American debtors to pay money owed to English creditors into the state treasury, and to pay it in paper money even though the paper had depreciated to 2 percent of its original value. Land use controls that rival modern zoning ordinances in their rigor regulated the use of property for slaughterhouses, bakeries, candle makers, and cemeteries. Many elements of economic life were closely regulated. Between 1781 and 1801, the New York legislature passed statutes regulating lotteries, peddlers, lenders, beggars, landlords, ferries, apprentices, dogs, fishermen, physicians, tavern owners, bakers, and (presumably in separate categories) bastards, idiots, lunatics, and lawyers. And none of this required any compensation of those whose economic interests were diminished or even extinguished by the government action. Both property law and theory and republican politics dictated the result: "The general good is to prevail over partial individual inconvenience," said the New York Supreme Court. Therefore, even when a city regraded a street and undermined the foundation of an adjoining house, or changed the course of a river resulting in its overflowing private land or obstructing access to private docks, no compensation was required.

Original Meaning of the Takings Clause

Then, why was the takings clause included in the Fifth Amendment, and what did it mean? Given the context, it could not be a crucial provision and integral to the constitutional scheme. Certainly, there was no great demand for it. The state conventions ratifying the Constitution proposed over eighty amendments to be included in the Bill of Rights, but the takings clause was not among them. If it was debated at all in the Congress that proposed the Bill of Rights or the states that ratified it, no record exists of that debate.

One thing that is clear from the contemporary commentaries is that the clause applied only to cases in which the government physically takes over a person's property. Even Justice [Antonin] Scalia, author of the leading contemporary property rights decision, admits that "early constitutional theorists did not believe that the Takings Clause embraced regulations of property at all." [James] Madison's original draft used a term that is as clear as "take": "No person shall be . . . obliged to relinquish his property, where it may be necessary for public use, without a just compensation." Beyond that, the clause only may have been designed to prevent particular confiscatory abuses, especially seizure of personal property by an army in the field. St. George Tucker, author of the first published legal commentary on the Bill of Rights, opined that the clause "was probably intended to restrain the arbitrary and oppressive mode of obtaining supplies for the army, and other public uses, by impressment, as was too frequently practiced during the revolutionary war, without any compensation whatever."

The Bill of Rights

CHAPTER 2

The Supreme Court and Eminent Domain

States Must Compensate Property Owners for Seized Property

John Marshall Harlan

In 1833 the Supreme Court heard the case of Barron v. Balti-more. *The case involved John Barron, who owned a wharf in Baltimore harbor. The expansion of the city resulted in the accumulation of sand deposits in the harbor, and Barron's business was no longer profitable without deep water. He sought compensation from the city for his losses. The case made its way to the Supreme Court, and Chief Justice John Marshall wrote a unanimous opinion that denied Barron any financial compensation. The Fifth Amendment's takings clause governed only federal government action, the Court declared, and did not require states or cities to pay just compensation before taking property.*

Sixty-four years later the Court decided Chicago, Burlington, and Quincey Railroad Company v. Chicago *(1897). The case involved Chicago's plan to widen a street. In order to accomplish the expansion, the city condemned parcels of land owned by individuals and parts of the railroad's right of way along the street. At a jury trial in which the jury set an amount of compensation to be paid, the jury awarded the railroad the sum of one dollar for the use of the right of way. The railroad appealed all the way to the U.S. Supreme Court.*

The Court, in an opinion authored by Justice John Marshall Harlan, determined that the Fourteenth Amendment applied to the state action in question. The Fourteenth Amendment, enacted in 1868, guaranteed due process of law in the states. Accordingly, whenever the state took property for private use, the taking had to be compensated properly or due process of law

John Marshall Harlan, Supreme Court decision in *Chicago, Burlington & Quincey Railroad Co. v. City of Chicago*, 166 U.S. 226, March 1, 1897.

would not be achieved. Thus, the Court affirmed that the rail-road was entitled to just compensation for the land taken by the state. However, the justices rejected the railroad's claim that one dollar was unjust compensation. The Court found that proper principles of law were applied, and the jury had properly fixed the compensation to be paid.

Justice John Marshall Harlan was one of the longest-serving justices on the Supreme Court. Starting in 1877, he served more than thirty-three years and earned the nickname "the Great Dissenter." Later, a grandson with the same name also served on the Supreme Court.

It is not contended—as it could not be—that the constitution of Illionis deprives the railroad company of any right secured by the fourteenth amendment. For the state constitution not only declares that no person shall be deprived of his property without due process of law, but that private property shall not be taken or damaged for public use without just compensation. But it must be observed that the prohibitions of the amendment refer to all the instrumentalities of the state—to its legislative, executive, and judicial authorities,— and therefore whoever, by virtue of public position under a state government, deprives another of any right protected by that amendment against deprivation by the state, 'violates the constitutional inhibition; and as he acts in the name and for the state, and is clothed with the state's power, his act is that of the state.' This must be so, or, as we have often said, the constitutional prohibition has no meaning, and 'the state has clothed one of its agents with power to annul or evade it.' Ex parte Virginia [1879]. These principles were enforced in the recent case of *Scott v. McNeal* [1894], in which it was held that the prohibitions of the fourteenth amendment extended to 'all acts of the state, whether through its legislative, its executive, or its judicial authorities'; and consequently it was held that a judgment of the highest court of a state, by which a purchaser at an administration sale, under an order of a probate court,

of land belonging to a living person who had not been noti-
fied of the proceedings, deprived him of his property without
due process of law, contrary to the fourteenth amendment.

State Court Action Must Meet Due Process Requirements

Nor is the contention that the railroad company has been deprived of its property without due process of law entirely met
by the suggestion that it had due notice of the proceedings for
condemnation, appeared in court, and was permitted to make
defense. It is true that this court has said that a trial in a court
of justice according to the modes of proceeding applicable to
such a case, secured by laws operating on all alike, and not
subjecting the individual to the arbitrary exercise of the powers of government unrestrained by the established principles
of private right and distributive justice,—the court having jurisdiction of the subject-matter and of the parties, and the defendant having full opportunity to be heard,—met the requirement of due process of law. But a state may not, by any
of its agencies, disregard the prohibitions of the fourteenth
amendment. Its judicial authorities may keep within the letter
of the statute prescribing forms of procedure in the courts,
and give the parties interested the fullest opportunity to be
heard, and yet it might be that its final action would be inconsistent with that amendment. In determining what is due
process of law, regard must be had to substance, not to form.
This court, referring to the fourteenth amendment, has said:
'Can a state make anything due process of law which, by its
own legislation, it chooses to declare such? To affirm this is to
hold that the prohibition to the states is of no avail, or has no
application, where the invasion of private rights is effected
under the forms of state legislation.' *Davidson v. New Orleans*
[1877]. The same question could be propounded, and the
same answer should be made, in reference to judicial proceedings inconsistent with the requirement of due process of law.

If compensation for private property taken for public use is an essential element of due process of law as ordained by the fourteenth amendment, then the final judgment of a state court, under the authority of which the property is in fact taken, is to be deemed the act of the state, within the meaning of that amendment.

Takings Must Be Compensated

It is proper now to inquire whether the due process of law enjoined by the fourteenth amendment requires compensation to be made or adequately secured to the owner of private property taken for public use under the authority of a state.

In *Davidson v. New Orleans*, above cited, it was said that a statute declaring in terms, without more, that the full and exclusive title to a described piece of land belonging to one person should be and is hereby vested in another person, would, if effectual, deprive the former of his property without due process of law, within the meaning of the fourteenth amendment. Such an enactment would not receive judicial sanction in any country having a written constitution distributing the powers of government among three coordinate departments, and committing to the judiciary, expressly or by implication, authority to enforce the provisions of such constitution. It would be treated, not as an exertion of legislative power, but as a sentence. . . . Due protection of the rights of property has been regarded as a vital principle of republican institutions. 'Next in degree to the right of personal liberty,' Mr. [Jacob] Broom, in his work on Constitutional Law, says, 'is that of enjoying private property without undue interference or molestation.' The requirement that the property shall not be taken for public use without just compensation is but 'an affirmance of a great doctrine established by the common law for the protection of private property. It is founded in natural equity, and is laid down as a principle of universal law. Indeed, in a free government, almost all other rights would become worthless if the government possessed an uncontrollable power over the private fortune of every citzen.'

But if, as this court has adjudged, a legislative enactment, assuming arbitrarily to take the property of one individual and give it to another individual, would not be due process of law, as enjoined by the fourteenth amendment, it must be that the requirement of due process of law in that amendment is applicable to the direct appropriation by the state to public use, and without compensation, of the private property of the citizen. The legislature may prescribe a form of procedure to be observed in the taking of private property for public use, but it is not due process of law if provision be not made for compensation. Notice to the owner to appear in some judicial tribunal and show cause why his property shall not be taken for public use without compensation would be a mockery of justice. Due process of law, as applied to judicial proceedings instituted for the taking of private property for public use means, therefore, such process as recognizes the right of the owner to be compensated if his property be wrested from him and transferred to the public. The mere form of the proceeding instituted against the owner, even if he be admitted to defend, cannot convert the process used into due process of law, if the necessary result be to deprive him of his property without compensation. . . .

In *Scott v. Toledo*, the late Mr. Justice [Howell E.] Jackson, while circuit judge, had occasion to consider this question. After full consideration that able judge said: 'Whatever may have been the power of the states on this subject prior to the adoption of the fourteenth amendment to the constitution, it seems clear that, since that amendment went into effect, such limitations and restraints have been placed upon their power in dealing with individual rights that the states cannot now lawfully appropriate private property for the public benefit or to public uses without compensation to the owner, and that any attempt so to do, whether done in pursuance of a constitutional provision or legislative enactment, whether done by the legislature itself or under delegated authority by one of the subordinate agencies of the state, and whether done directly, by taking the property of one person and vesting it in another or the public, or indirectly, through the forms of law, by appropriating the property and requiring the owner thereof to compensate himself, or to refund to another the compensation to which he is entitled, would be wanting in that 'due process of law' required by said amendment. The conclusion of the court on this question is that, since the adoption of the fourteenth amendment, compensation for private property taken for public uses constitutes an essential element in 'due process of law,' and that without such compensation the appropriation of private property to public uses, no matter under what form of procedure it is taken, would violate the provisions of the federal constitution. . . .

In our opinion, a judgment of a state court, even if it be authorized by statute, whereby private property is taken for the state or under its direction for public use, without compensation made or secured to the owner, is, upon principle and authority, wanting in the due process of law required by the fourteenth amendment of the constitution of the United States, and the affirmance of such judgment by the highest court of the state is a denial by that state of a right secured to the owner by that instrument.

The Jury Properly Determined the Compensation Due

It remains to inquire whether the necessary effect of the proceedings in the court below was to appropriate to the public use any property right of the railroad company without compensation being made or secured to the owner.

The contention of the railroad company is that the verdict and judgment for one dollar as the amount to be paid to it was, in effect, an appropriation of its property rights without any compensation whatever; that the judgment should be read as if, in form as well as in fact, it made no provision whatever for compensation for the property so appropriated.

Undoubtedly the verdict may not unreasonably be taken as meaning that in the judgment of the jury the company's property, proposed to be taken, was not materially damaged; that is, looking at the nature of the property, and the purposes for which it was obtained and was being used, that which was taken from the company was not, in the judgment of the jury, of any substantial value in money. The owner of private property taken under the right of eminent domain obtains just compensation if he is awarded such sum as, under all the circumstances, is a fair and full equivalent for the thing taken from him by the public.

If the opening of the street across the railroad tracks did not unduly interfere with the company's use of the right of way for legitimate railroad purposes, then its compensation would be nominal. But whether there was such an interference, what was its extent, and what was the value of that lost by the company as the direct result of such interference, were questions of fact, which the state committed to the jury under such instructions touching the law as were proper and necessary. It was for the jury to determine the facts, but it belonged to the court to detemine the legal principles by which they were to be governed in fixing the amount of compensation to the owner. . . .

The expenses that will be incurred by the railroad company in erecting gates, planking the crossing, and maintaining flagmen, in order that its road may be safely operated—if all that should be required—necessarily result from the maintenance of a public highway under legislative sanction, and must be deemed to have been taken by the company into account when it accepted the privileges and franchises granted by the state. Such expenses must be regarded as incidental to the exercise of the police powers of the state. What was obtained, and all that was obtained, by the condemnation proceedings for the public was the right to open a street across land within the crossing that was used, and was always likely to be used, for railroad tracks. While the city was bound to make compensation for that which was actually taken, it cannot be required to compensate the defendant for obeying lawful regulations enacted for the safety of the lives and property of the people. And the value to the railroad company of that which was taken from it is . . . , the difference between the value of the right to the exclusive use of the land in question for the purposes for which it was being used, and for which it was always likely to be used, and that value after the city acquired the privilege of participating in such use by the opening of a street across it, leaving the railroad tracks untouched. Upon that theory the case was considered by the jury, and the court did not err in placing it before them upon that basis as to compensation.

Rent-Control Laws Are Not a Form of Property Seizure

Sandra Day O'Connor

The following selection is excerpted from the U.S. Supreme Court's ruling in Yee v. City of Escondido *(1992), authored by Justice Sandra Day O'Connor. The case centered on a local rent-control ordinance affecting mobile home parks in California. John and Irene Yee, the owners of two mobile home parks, sued the city on the grounds that the rent-control law amounted to a taking because it effectively gave tenants the right to permanently occupy their property. Their case was dismissed by a lower court, and the Yees appealed to the Supreme Court.*

The Supreme Court affirmed the lower court's decision. As O'Connor states in the following excerpt, the ordinance was not a seizure of property since it did not result in the forced physical occupation of the Yees' land. The law amounted to only a regulation of land use, not an actual taking of property. Thus, the Court clearly distinguished between government regulation of private property, which is constitutional, and taking of property, which violates the Fifth Amendment.

Sandra Day O'Connor was appointed by President Ronald Reagan and was unanimously confirmed by the Senate as the first female justice on the U.S. Supreme Court. In a centrist position on the Court, she often became the fifth—and deciding—vote with the Court's conservative bloc. Accordingly, many people consider her one of the most influential women in America's history. After nearly twenty-five years on the Court, she retired in January 2006.

The Takings Clause of the Fifth Amendment provides: "[N]or shall private property be taken for public use, without just compensation." Most of our cases interpreting

Sandra Day O'Connor, U.S. Supreme Court decision in *Yee v. City of Escondido*, 503 U.S. 519, 1992.

the Clause fall within two distinct classes. Where the government authorizes a physical occupation of property (or actually takes title), the Takings Clause generally requires compensation. But where the government merely regulates the use of property, compensation is required only if considerations such as the purpose of the regulation or the extent to which it deprives the owner of the economic use of the property suggest that the regulation has unfairly singled out the property owner to bear a burden that should be borne by the public as a whole. The first category of cases requires courts to apply a clear rule; the second necessarily entails complex factual assessments of the purposes and economic effects of government actions.

Petitioners [the Yees] own mobile home parks in Escondido, California. They contend that a local rent control ordinance, when viewed against the backdrop of California's Mobilehome Residency Law, amounts to a physical occupation of their property, entitling them to compensation under the first category of cases discussed above.

The Mobilehome Residency Law

The term "mobile home" is somewhat misleading. Mobile homes are largely immobile as a practical matter, because the cost of moving one is often a significant fraction of the value of the mobile home itself. They are generally placed permanently in parks; once in place, only about 1 in every 100 mobile homes is ever moved. A mobile home owner typically rents a plot of land, called a "pad," from the owner of a mobile home park. The park owner provides private roads within the park, common facilities such as washing machines or a swimming pool, and often utilities. The mobile home owner often invests in site-specific improvements such as a driveway, steps, walkways, porches, or landscaping. When the mobile home owner wishes to move, the mobile home is usually sold in place, and the purchaser continues to rent the pad on which the mobile home is located.

In 1978, California enacted its Mobilehome Residency Law, Cal.Civ.Code Ann. 798 et seq. The legislature found "that, because of the high cost of moving mobilehomes, the potential for damage resulting therefrom, the requirements relating to the installation of mobilehomes, and the cost of landscaping or lot preparation, it is necessary that the owners of mobilehomes occupied within mobilehome parks be provided with the unique protection from actual or constructive eviction afforded by the provisions of this chapter."

The Mobilehome Residency Law limits the bases upon which a park owner may terminate a mobile home owner's tenancy. These include the nonpayment of rent, the mobile home owner's violation of law or park rules, and the park owner's desire to change the use of his land. While a rental agreement is in effect, however, the park owner generally may not require the removal of a mobile home when it is sold. The park owner may neither charge a transfer fee for the sale, nor disapprove of the purchaser, provided that the purchaser has the ability to pay the rent. The Mobilehome Residency Law contains a number of other detailed provisions, but none limit the rent the park owner may charge.

The Rent Control Ordinance

In the wake of the Mobilehome Residency Law, various communities in California adopted mobile home rent control ordinances. The voters of Escondido did the same in 1988 by approving Proposition K, the rent control ordinance challenged here. The ordinance sets rents back to their 1986 levels and prohibits rent increases without the approval of the city council. Park owners may apply to the council for rent increases at any time. The council must approve any increases it determines to be "just, fair and reasonable." ...

The Lawsuit and Appellate Route

Petitioners John and Irene Yee own the Friendly Hills and Sunset Terrace Mobile Home Parks, both of which are located in the city of Escondido. A few months after the adoption of Escondido's rent control ordinance, they filed suit in San Diego County Superior Court. According to the complaint, "[t]he rent control law has had the effect of depriving the plaintiffs of all use and occupancy of [their] real property and granting to the tenants of mobilehomes presently in The Park, as well as the successors in interest of such tenants, the right to physically permanently occupy and use the real property of Plaintiff." The Yees requested damages of 6 million dollars, a declaration that the rent control ordinance is unconstitutional, and an injunction barring the ordinance's enforcement. . . .

The Superior Court nevertheless sustained the city's demurrer and dismissed the Yees' complaint.

The Yees were not alone. Eleven other park owners filed similar suits against the city shortly afterwards, and all were dismissed. By stipulation, all 12 cases were consolidated for appeal; the parties agreed that all would be submitted for decision by the California Court of Appeal on the briefs and oral argument in the Yee case.

The Court of Appeal affirmed. . . . The California Supreme Court denied review.

Eight of the twelve park owners, including the Yees, joined in a petition for certiorari. We granted certiorari. . . .

The Yees' Argument

Petitioners do not claim that the ordinary rent control statutes regulating housing throughout the country violate the Takings Clause. Instead, their argument is predicated on the unusual economic relationship between park owners and mobile home owners. Park owners may no longer set rents or decide who their tenants will be. As a result, according to petitioners, any reduction in the rent for a mobile home pad causes a corresponding increase in the value of a mobile home, because the mobile home owner now owns, in addition to a mobile home, the right to occupy a pad at a rent below the value that would be set by the free market. Because, under the California Mobilehome Residency Law, the park owner cannot evict a mobile home owner or easily convert the property to other uses, the argument goes, the mobile home owner is effectively a perpetual tenant of the park, and the increase in the mobile home's value thus represents the right to occupy a pad at below-market rent indefinitely. And because the Mobilehome Residency Law permits the mobile home owner to sell the mobile home in place, the mobile home owner can receive a premium from the purchaser corresponding to this increase in value. The amount of this premium is not limited by the Mobilehome Residency Law or the Escondido ordinance. As a result, petitioners conclude, the rent control ordinance has transferred a discrete interest in land—the right to occupy the land indefinitely at a submarket rent—from the park owner to the mobile home owner. Petitioners contend that what has been transferred from park owner to mobile home owner is no less than a right of physical occupation of the park owner's land.

Rent Control is Not a Physical Taking

This argument, while perhaps within the scope of our regulatory taking cases, cannot be squared easily with our cases on physical takings. The government effects a physical taking only where it requires the landowner to submit to the physical occupation of his land. "This element of required acquiescence is at the heart of the concept of occupation." *FCC v. Florida Power Corp.* (1987). Thus whether the government floods a landowner's property, or does no more than require the landowner to suffer the installation of a cable, the Takings Clause requires compensation if the government authorizes a compelled physical invasion of property.

But the Escondido rent control ordinance, even when considered in conjunction with the California Mobilehome Residency Law, authorizes no such thing. Petitioners voluntarily rented their land to mobile home owners. At least on the face of the regulatory scheme, neither the city nor the State compels petitioners, once they have rented their property to tenants, to continue doing so. To the contrary, the Mobilehome Residency Law provides that a park owner who wishes to change the use of his land may evict his tenants, albeit with 6 or 12 months notice. Put bluntly, no government has required any physical invasion of petitioners' property. Petitioners' tenants were invited by petitioners, not forced upon them by the government. While the "right to exclude" is doubtless, as petitioners assert, "one of the most essential sticks in the bundle of rights that are commonly characterized as property," *Kaiser Aetna v. United States* (1979), we do not find that right to have been taken from petitioners on the mere face of the Escondido ordinance.

Petitioners suggest that the statutory procedure for changing the use of a mobile home park is in practice "a kind of gauntlet," in that they are not in fact free to change the use of their land. Because petitioners do not claim to have run that gauntlet, however, this case provides no occasion to consider how the procedure has been applied to petitioners' property, and we accordingly confine ourselves to the face of the statute. . . .

The Laws Regulate Land Use

On their face, the state and local laws at issue here merely regulate petitioners' use of their land by regulating the relationship between landlord and tenant. "This Court has consistently affirmed that States have broad power to regulate housing conditions in general, and the landlord-tenant relationship in particular, without paying compensation for all economic injuries that such regulation entails." [*Loretto v. Teleprompter* (1982)]. . . . When a landowner decides to rent his land to tenants, the government may place ceilings on the rents the landowner can charge, or require the landowner to accept tenants he does not like, without automatically having to pay compensation. . . .

Petitioners emphasize that the ordinance transfers wealth from park owners to incumbent [existing] mobile home owners. Other forms of land use regulation, however, can also be said to transfer wealth from the one who is regulated to another. Ordinary rent control often transfers wealth from landlords to tenants by reducing the landlords' income and the tenants' monthly payments, although it does not cause a one-time transfer of value, as occurs with mobile homes. Traditional zoning regulations can transfer wealth from those whose activities are prohibited to their neighbors; when a property owner is barred from mining coal on his land, for example, the value of his property may decline, but the value of his neighbor's property may rise. The mobile home owner's ability to sell the mobile home at a premium may make this wealth transfer more visible than in the ordinary case, but the existence of the transfer in itself does not convert regulation into physical invasion.

No Forced Physical Occupation

Petitioners also rely heavily on their allegation that the ordinance benefits incumbent mobile home owners without benefiting future mobile home owners, who will be forced to purchase mobile homes at premiums. Mobile homes, like motor vehicles, ordinarily decline in value with age. But the effect of the rent control ordinance, coupled with the restrictions on the park owner's freedom to reject new tenants, is to increase significantly the value of the mobile home. This increased value normally benefits only the tenant in possession at the time the rent control is imposed. Petitioners are correct in citing the existence of this premium as a difference between the alleged effect of the Escondido ordinance and that of an ordinary apartment rent control statute. Most apartment tenants do not sell anything to their successors, . . . so a typical rent control statute will transfer wealth from the landlord to the incumbent tenant and all future tenants. By contrast, petitioners contend that the Escondido ordinance transfers wealth only to the incumbent mobile home owner. This effect might have some bearing on whether the ordinance causes a regulatory taking, as it may shed some light on whether there is a sufficient nexus between the effect of the ordinance and the objectives it is supposed to advance. But it has nothing to do with whether the ordinance causes a physical taking. Whether the ordinance benefits only current mobile home owners or all mobile home owners, it does not require petitioners to submit to the physical occupation of their land.

The same may be said of petitioners' contention that the ordinance amounts to compelled physical occupation because it deprives petitioners of the ability to choose their incoming tenants. Again, this effect may be relevant to a regulatory taking argument, as it may be one factor a reviewing court would wish to consider in determining whether the ordinance unjustly imposes a burden on petitioners that should "be compensated by the government, rather than remain[ing] disproportionately concentrated on a few persons." *Penn Central Transporatation Co. v. New York City.* But it does not convert regulation into the unwanted physical occupation of land. Because they voluntarily open their property to occupation by others, petitioners cannot assert a per se right to compensation based on their inability to exclude particular individuals. . . .

The Escondido rent control ordinance, even considered against the backdrop of California's Mobilehome Residency Law, does not authorize an unwanted physical occupation of petitioners' property. It is a regulation of petitioners' use of their property, and thus does not amount to a per se taking.

Taking Property for Economic Development Is Constitutional

John Paul Stevens

The U.S. Supreme Court case Kelo v. City of New London
*(2005) involved an economic development plan that was meant
to revitalize part of the city of New London, Connecticut. The
city had purchased most of the property needed to implement
the plan. However, Susette Kelo and a few other owners refused
to sell. In response, the city brought condemnation proceedings to
take the property. Kelo and the other owners in turn brought a
legal action to permanently prevent New London from taking
their properties. The trial court issued an order that prohibited
the taking of some of the disputed properties. However, on appeal, the Connecticut Superior Court reversed that determination and permitted New London to take all of the properties in
question. The U.S. Supreme Court took the case in order to examine whether taking private property for the purpose of economic development was justified under the takings clause of the
Fifth Amendment.*

*In an opinion written by John Paul Stevens, excerpted here,
the Court upheld the lower court's ruling that the takings were
justified. Stevens explained that the Court has traditionally
broadly interpreted the term* public use *in the Fifth Amendment. Thus, it is not only legitimate to take property for traditional public uses such as highways and railroads, but it is also
permissible to take private property for public purposes such as
economic improvement that will benefit society in general. Furthermore, there is no need for New London to show that the economic development plan will occur with "reasonable certainty"
before the takings can occur. However, the Court left open the
possibility that states may impose "public use" requirements that*

John Paul Stevens, Supreme Court decision in *Susette Kelo, et al., Petitioners v. City of New London, Connecticut, et al.*, June 23, 2005.

*are stricter than the Court's broad interpretation of the defini-
tion under the Fifth Amendment.*

*Justice John Paul Stevens has served on the Supreme Court
for more than thirty years. He is the Court's oldest member and
the longest-serving sitting judge.*

In 2000, the city of New London approved a development plan that, in the words of the Supreme Court of Connecticut, was "projected to create in excess of 1,000 jobs, to increase tax and other revenues, and to revitalize an economically distressed city, including its downtown and waterfront areas." In assembling the land needed for this project, the city's development agent has purchased property from willing sellers and proposes to use the power of eminent domain to acquire the remainder of the property from unwilling owners in exchange for just compensation. The question presented is whether the city's proposed disposition of this property qualifies as a "public use" within the meaning of the Takings Clause of the Fifth Amendment to the Constitution. . . .

Lower Court Rulings

In December 2000, petitioners [Susette Kelo and others] brought this action in the New London Superior Court. They claimed, among other things, that the taking of their properties would violate the "public use" restriction in the Fifth Amendment. After a 7-day bench trial, the Superior Court granted a permanent restraining order prohibiting the taking of the properties located in parcel 4A [of the redevelopment plan] (park or marina support). It, however, denied petitioners relief as to the properties located in parcel 3 (office space).

After the Superior Court ruled, both sides took appeals to the Supreme Court of Connecticut. That court held, over a dissent, that all of the City's proposed takings were valid. It began by upholding the lower court's determination that the takings were authorized by chapter 132, the State's municipal development statute. That statute expresses a legislative determination that the taking of land, even developed land, as part of an economic development project is a "public use" and in the "public interest." Next, relying on [U.S. Supreme Court] cases such as *Hawaii Housing Authority v. Midkiff* (1984), and *Berman v. Parker* (1954), the court held that such economic development qualified as a valid public use under both the Federal and State Constitutions.

Finally, adhering to its precedents, the court went on to determine, first, whether the takings of the particular properties at issue were "reasonably necessary" to achieving the City's intended public use, and, second, whether the takings were for "reasonably foreseeable needs." The court upheld the trial court's factual findings as to parcel 3, but reversed the trial court as to parcel 4A, agreeing with the City that the intended use of this land was sufficiently definite and had been given "reasonable attention" during the planning process.

The three dissenting justices would have imposed a "heightened" standard of judicial review for takings justified by economic development. Although they agreed that the plan was intended to serve a valid public use, they would have found all the takings unconstitutional because the City had failed to adduce "clear and convincing evidence" that the economic benefits of the plan would in fact come to pass.

We granted certiorari to determine whether a city's decision to take property for the purpose of economic development satisfies the "public use" requirement of the Fifth Amendment.

Public Use vs. Public Purpose

Two polar propositions are perfectly clear. On the one hand, it has long been accepted that the sovereign [government] may not take the property of *A* for the sole purpose of transferring it to another private party *B*, even though *A* is paid just compensation. On the other hand, it is equally clear that a State may transfer property from one private party to another if future "use by the public" is the purpose of the taking; the condemnation of land for a railroad with common-carrier duties is a familiar example. Neither of these propositions, however, determines the disposition of this case.

As for the first proposition, the City would no doubt be forbidden from taking petitioners' land for the purpose of conferring a private benefit on a particular private party.... Nor would the City be allowed to take property under the mere pretext of a public purpose, when its actual purpose was to bestow a private benefit. The takings before us, however, would be executed pursuant to a "carefully considered" development plan. The trial judge and all the members of the Supreme Court of Connecticut agreed that there was no evidence of an illegitimate purpose in this case. Therefore, as was true of the statute challenged in *Midkiff*, the City's development plan was not adopted "to benefit a particular class of identifiable individuals."

On the other hand, this is not a case in which the City is planning to open the condemned land—at least not in its entirety—to use by the general public. Nor will the private lessees of the land in any sense be required to operate like common carriers, making their services available to all comers. But although such a projected use would be sufficient to satisfy the public use requirement, this "Court long ago rejected any literal requirement that condemned property be put into use for the general public." [*Midkiff*] Indeed, while many state courts in the mid-19th century endorsed "use by the public" as the proper definition of public use, that narrow view steadily eroded over time. Not only was the "use by the public" test difficult to administer (*e.g.*, what proportion of the public need have access to the property? at what price?), but it proved to be impractical given the diverse and always evolving needs of society. Accordingly, when this Court began applying the Fifth Amendment to the States at the close of the 19th century, it embraced the broader and more natural interpretation of public use as "public purpose." Thus, in a case upholding a mining company's use of an aerial bucket line to transport ore over property it did not own, Justice [Oliver Wendell] Holmes' opinion for the Court stressed "the inadequacy of use by the general public as a universal test." *Strickley v. Highland Boy Gold Mining Co.*, (1906). We have repeatedly and consistently rejected that narrow test ever since.

The disposition of this case therefore turns on the question whether the City's development plan serves a "public purpose." Without exception, our cases have defined that concept broadly, reflecting our longstanding policy of deference to legislative judgments in this field.

"Public Purpose" Precedent

In *Berman v. Parker* (1954), this Court upheld a redevelopment plan targeting a blighted area of Washington, D.C., in which most of the housing for the area's 5,000 inhabitants was beyond repair. Under the plan, the area would be condemned and part of it utilized for the construction of streets, schools, and other public facilities. The remainder of the land would be leased or sold to private parties for the purpose of redevelopment, including the construction of low-cost housing.

The owner of a department store located in the area challenged the condemnation, pointing out that his store was not itself blighted and arguing that the creation of a "better balanced, more attractive community" was not a valid public use. Writing for a unanimous Court, Justice [William] Douglas refused to evaluate this claim in isolation, deferring instead to the legislative and agency judgment that the area "must be planned as a whole" for the plan to be successful. The Court explained that "community redevelopment programs need not, by force of the Constitution, be on a piecemeal basis—lot by lot, building by building." The public use underlying the taking was unequivocally affirmed. . . .

In *Hawaii Housing Authority v. Midkiff* (1984), the Court considered a Hawaii statute whereby fee title was taken from lessors and transferred to lessees (for just compensation) in order to reduce the concentration of land ownership. We unanimously upheld the statute and rejected the Ninth Circuit's view that it was "a naked attempt on the part of the state of Hawaii to take the property of A and transfer it to B solely for B's private use and benefit." Reaffirming *Berman's* deferential approach to legislative judgments in this field, we concluded that the State's purpose of eliminating the "social and economic evils of a land oligopoly" qualified as a valid public use. Our opinion also rejected the contention that the mere fact that the State immediately transferred the properties to private individuals upon condemnation somehow diminished the public character of the taking. "[I]t is only the taking's purpose, and not its mechanics," we explained, that matters in determining public use.

In that same Term we decided another public use case that arose in a purely economic context. In *Ruckelshaus v. Monsanto Co.* (1984), the Court dealt with provisions of the Federal Insecticide, Fungicide, and Rodenticide Act under which the Environmental Protection Agency could consider the data (including trade secrets) submitted by a prior pesticide applicant in evaluating a subsequent application, so long as the second applicant paid just compensation for the data. We acknowledged that the "most direct beneficiaries" of these provisions were the subsequent applicants, but we nevertheless upheld the statute under *Berman* and *Midkiff*. We found sufficient Congress' belief that sparing applicants the cost of time-consuming research eliminated a significant barrier to entry in the pesticide market and thereby enhanced competition.

Viewed as a whole, our jurisprudence has recognized that the needs of society have varied between different parts of the Nation, just as they have evolved over time in response to changed circumstances. Our earliest cases in particular embodied a strong theme of federalism, emphasizing the "great respect" that we owe to state legislatures and state courts in discerning local public needs. . . . For more than a century, our public use jurisprudence has wisely eschewed rigid formulas and intrusive scrutiny in favor of affording legislatures broad latitude in determining what public needs justify the use of the takings power.

Economic Development Is a Legitimate Public Purpose

Those who govern the City were not confronted with the need to remove blight in the Fort Trumbull area, but their determination that the area was sufficiently distressed to justify a program of economic rejuvenation is entitled to our deference. The City has carefully formulated an economic development plan that it believes will provide appreciable benefits to the community, including—but by no means limited to—new jobs and increased tax revenue. As with other exercises in urban planning and development, the City is endeavoring to coordinate a variety of commercial, residential, and recreational uses of land, with the hope that they will form a whole greater than the sum of its parts. To effectuate this plan, the City has invoked a state statute that specifically authorizes the use of eminent domain to promote economic development. Given the comprehensive character of the plan, the thorough deliberation that preceded its adoption, and the limited scope of our review, it is appropriate for us, as it was in *Berman*, to resolve the challenges of the individual owners, not on a piecemeal basis, but rather in light of the entire plan. Because that plan unquestionably serves a public purpose, the takings challenged here satisfy the public use requirement of the Fifth Amendment.

To avoid this result, petitioners urge us to adopt a new bright-line rule that economic development does not qualify as a public use. Putting aside the unpersuasive suggestion that the City's plan will provide only purely economic benefits, neither precedent nor logic supports petitioners' proposal. Promoting economic development is a traditional and long accepted function of government. There is, moreover, no principled way of distinguishing economic development from the other public purposes that we have recognized. In our cases upholding takings that facilitated agriculture and mining, for example, we emphasized the importance of those industries to the welfare of the States in question; in *Berman*, we endorsed the purpose of transforming a blighted area into a "well-balanced" community through redevelopment; in *Midkiff*, we upheld the interest in breaking up a land oligopoly that "created artificial deterrents to the normal functioning of the State's residential land market"; and in *Monsanto*, we accepted Congress' purpose of eliminating a "significant barrier to entry in the pesticide market." It would be incongruous to hold that the City's interest in the economic benefits to be derived from the development of the Fort Trumbull area has less of a public character than any of those other interests. Clearly, there is no basis for exempting economic development from our traditionally broad understanding of public purpose.

Benefiting Private Parties

Petitioners contend that using eminent domain for economic development impermissibly blurs the boundary between public and private takings. Again, our cases foreclose this objection. Quite simply, the government's pursuit of a public purpose will often benefit individual private parties. For example, in *Midkiff*, the forced transfer of property conferred a direct and significant benefit on those lessees who were previously unable to purchase their homes. In *Monsanto*, we recognized that the "most direct beneficiaries" of the data-sharing provisions were the subsequent pesticide applicants, but benefiting them in this way was necessary to promoting competition in the pesticide market. The owner of the department store in *Berman* objected to "taking from one businessman for the benefit of another businessman," referring to the fact that under the redevelopment plan land would be leased or sold to private developers for redevelopment. Our rejection of that contention [in *Berman*] has particular relevance to the instant case: "The public end may be as well or better served through an agency of private enterprise than through a department of government—or so the Congress might conclude. We cannot say that public ownership is the sole method of promoting the public purposes of community redevelopment projects."

It is further argued that without a bright-line rule nothing would stop a city from transferring citizen *A*'s property to citizen *B* for the sole reason that citizen *B* will put the property to a more productive use and thus pay more taxes. Such a one-to-one transfer of property, executed outside the confines of an integrated development plan, is not presented in this case. While such an unusual exercise of government power would certainly raise a suspicion that a private purpose was afoot, the hypothetical cases posited by petitioners can be confronted if and when they arise. They do not warrant the crafting of an artificial restriction on the concept of public use.

A "Reasonable Certainty" of Use Is Not Required

Alternatively, petitioners maintain that for takings of this kind we should require a "reasonable certainty" that the expected public benefits will actually accrue. Such a rule, however, would represent an even greater departure from our precedent. "When the legislature's purpose is legitimate and its means are not irrational, our cases make clear that empirical debates over the wisdom of takings—no less than debates over the wisdom of other kinds of socioeconomic legislation—are not to be carried out in the federal courts."

Midkiff. . . . The disadvantages of a heightened form of review are especially pronounced in this type of case. Orderly implementation of a comprehensive redevelopment plan obviously requires that the legal rights of all interested parties be established before new construction can be commenced. A constitutional rule that required postponement of the judicial approval of every condemnation until the likelihood of success of the plan had been assured would unquestionably impose a significant impediment to the successful consummation of many such plans.

Just as we decline to second-guess the City's considered judgments about the efficacy of its development plan, we also decline to second-guess the City's determinations as to what lands it needs to acquire in order to effectuate the project. "It is not for the courts to oversee the choice of the boundary line nor to sit in review on the size of a particular project area. Once the question of the public purpose has been decided, the amount and character of land to be taken for the project and the need for a particular tract to complete the integrated plan rests in the discretion of the legislative branch." *Berman.*

States May Take Stricter Measures

In affirming the City's authority to take petitioners' properties, we do not minimize the hardship that condemnations may entail, notwithstanding the payment of just compensation. We emphasize that nothing in our opinion precludes any State from placing further restrictions on its exercise of the takings power. Indeed, many States already impose "public use" requirements that are stricter than the federal baseline. Some of these requirements have been established as a matter of state constitutional law, while others are expressed in state eminent domain statutes that carefully limit the grounds upon which takings may be exercised. As the submissions of the parties and their *amici* [friend of the court briefs] make clear, the necessity and wisdom of using eminent domain to promote economic development are certainly matters of legitimate public debate. This Court's authority, however, extends only to determining whether the City's proposed condemnations are for a "public use" within the meaning of the Fifth Amendment to the Federal Constitution. Because over a century of our case law interpreting that provision dictates an affirmative answer to that question, we may not grant petitioners the relief that they seek.

Private Property Should Not Be Taken for Economic Development

Jeff Jacoby

In the following selection Boston Globe columnist Jeff Jacoby criticizes the decision in Kelo v. City of New London *in which the U.S. Supreme Court ruled that it was constitutional for a city to take people's private property for the purposes of economic redevelopment. He contends that the Court has misinterpreted the phrase* public use *in the takings clause of the Fifth Amendment to mean that the government can take property even if most of the benefit will go to private developers rather than to the public. In addition, he highlights the views of the four dissenting justices, who argue that the Kelo decision will disproportionately harm the poor and minorities since they are more likely than others to be forced from their homes through eminent domain.*

I reached Mike Cristofaro on Thursday afternoon, a few hours after the Supreme Court ruled that local governments can seize people's property by eminent domain and turn it over to private developers. The court's 5-4 decision was a defeat for seven New London, Conn., property owners, who have resisted the city's plan to demolish their homes to make way for offices, upscale condos, and a waterfront hotel. Mike's 79-year-old father, Pasquale Cristofaro, is one of those homeowners, and I wondered how he had taken the news.

"I haven't told my father yet," Mike said. "I don't know what to say. You want to help me break it to him?"

Jeff Jacoby, "Eminent Injustice in New London," *The Boston Globe*, June 26, 2005. Republished with permission of The Boston Globe, conveyed through Copyright Clearance Center, Inc.

A Loyal Employee is Forced Out

I first met the Cristofaros in July 2001. The homeowners' lawsuit against the city was going to trial, and I'd come to New London to talk to some of the plaintiffs and see their homes in the Fort Trumbull neighborhood for myself. As Mike and I walked to his parents' home on Goshen Street, he recalled how they had learned that the city intended to force them from their property. On the day before Thanksgiving, a sheriff's deputy had shown up at their front door with condemnation papers and ordered them to be out by March. The news came as such a shock that Mike's mother, Margerita, began having heart palpitations and had to be taken to the hospital. (She passed away in 2003.)

For 27 years, Pasquale had been a loyal city employee. But no one from the New London Development Corp.—the agency charged with transforming the area into a fashionable complement to the big research headquarters Pfizer was building nearby—ever came to talk with the Cristofaros about the city's interest in their property. No one from City Hall asked the elderly couple if there was anything that might make a relocation less traumatic. Like the other homeowners, they were told just one thing: Sell now or be forced out.

"These people don't have no respect," Pasquale, who immigrated from Italy in 1962, told me that day. "You supposed to go like gentlemen—make me a price, ask me a yes or no. I love this house. I pay my bill, I pay the tax. And now they say I should get out? It's not right. It's not right."

No, it's not right. But five Supreme Court justices have just said it's constitutional.

Eviscerating the Public Use Clause

In effect, the majority in *Kelo v. New London* held that the words "public use" in the Fifth Amendment—"nor shall private property be taken for *public use* without just compensation"—can mean wholly private use, so long as the government expects it to yield some incidental public benefit—more tax revenue, new jobs, "maybe even aesthetic pleasure," as Justice Sandra Day O'Connor wrote in a dissent joined by Chief Justice William Rehnquist and justices Antonin Scalia and Clarence Thomas. Would your town's tax base grow if your home were bulldozed and replaced with a parking garage? If so, it may not be your home for long.

As a result of this evisceration of the Public Use clause, "the specter of condemnation hangs over all property," the dissenters warn. "Nothing is to prevent the state from replacing any Motel 6 with a Ritz-Carlton, any home with a shopping mall, or any farm with a factory."

In truth, though, it isn't *all* property that is at risk. If "public use" now means the government can evict a property owner so that a new owner can use the land to make more money, it is clear who will suffer most. "The fallout from this decision will not be random," O'Connor wrote sadly. "The beneficiaries are likely to be those citizens with disproportionate influence and power in the political process, including large corporations and development firms. . . . The government now has license to transfer property from those with fewer resources to those with more."

In a separate dissent, Thomas made the same point: "These losses will fall disproportionately on poor communities . . . the least politically powerful." Fifty years of eminent domain statistics drive home the fact that families uprooted by eminent domain tend to be nonwhite and/or nonwealthy. No wonder urban renewal came to be known bitterly as "Negro removal."

Living With the Consequences

"These five justices," Mike Cristofaro told me, "I hope someone looks at their property and says, 'You know, we could put that land to better use—why don't we get the town to take it from them by eminent domain.' Then maybe they would understand what they're putting my father through."

That won't happen. It isn't the high and mighty on whom avaricious governments and developers prey. Justices John Paul Stevens, Stephen Breyer, David Souter, Ruth Bader Ginsburg, and Anthony Kennedy are responsible for this execrable decision. But they'll never have to live with its consequences.

CHAPTER 3

The Bill
of Rights

The Supreme Court
and Regulatory Takings

Regulatory Takings Under the Rehnquist Court

Mark Tushnet

The Supreme Court has recognized two types of takings under the Fifth Amendment. In a physical taking, the government takes the property it needs and compensates the owner through the process of eminent domain. In a regulatory taking, government regulations on land use are deemed so excessive that they effectively deprive the property of its value, so the government must compensate the owner. Determining what constitutes a physical taking is straightforward. However, defining what regulations amount to a regulatory taking is less clear-cut and has led to a great deal of debate.

In the following selection Mark Tushnet argues that during the era of Supreme Court chief justice William Rehnquist, conservative justices attempted to expand the definition of a regulatory taking in an effort to impede government regulation of property. He summarizes the three most important cases in this area: Penn Central Transportation Company v. the City of New York *(1978),* Lucas v. South Carolina Coastal Council *(1992), and* Palazzolo v. Rhode Island *(2001). Tushnet concludes that although the Takings Project did not eradicate government regulation of property, it did make regulation more expensive. As developers realized they could start long-term lawsuits to challenge the laws, it cost governing authorities more money to try to implement their regulations.*

Mark Tushnet is a professor at Georgetown University Law Center and the author of A Court Divided: The Rehnquist Court and the Future of Constitutional Law.

Mark Tushnet, *A Court Divided: The Rehnquist Court and the Future of Constitutional Law.* New York: W.W. Norton & Company, 2005. Copyright © 2005 by Mark Tushnet. All rights reserved. Used by permission of W. W. Norton & Company, Inc.

The takings clause says that governments can't take your property unless they give you "just compensation" for it. It means that the government can buy your property from you even if you don't want to sell it and can pay you a fair market price rather than the price you would charge if you *did* want to sell. Government takings are most familiar in connection with the power of eminent domain. The government has a project it wants to pursue—build a convention center, for example—and it needs to assemble the land for the project. It wouldn't be fair for the government simply to seize the property it wanted because that would give the whole city or state the benefit of getting the convention center at the expense of the individual property owner. So the government has to pay for the land it takes. But we can't run a government that assembles land for projects by allowing property owners to set their own prices for the property. The convention center has to be built at a particular place, and the landowners, particularly the owner of the very last piece of land needed for the project, could blackmail the city into paying outrageous prices for the parcels. That's why the government has the power to take property over an owner's objection, why the government has to pay something for the property, and why the price is the fair market value and not what the landowner might like to bargain for.

The example of taking land for a convention center through the power of eminent domain illustrates both the historical core of the takings clause and its common sense. Traditional cases cropped up occasionally on the [Chief Justice William] Rehnquist Court's docket, but they really didn't matter much to real estate developers and business interests. Developers were much more concerned with modern land use regulations. Historic preservation statutes blocked the projects they wanted to pursue, and some towns and cities forced developers to give up some of their property to create parks and other recreation areas in exchange for permission to develop subdivisions. . . . Developers were concerned about environmental regulations too. Moreover, as the modern environmental movement matured, states and cities began to adopt smart growth programs that imposed additional limits on real estate development. Business interests were more generally concerned about extensive regulation, the modern versions of the regulations their predecessors had challenged as violations of substantive due process.

The traditional idea of the takings clause didn't help in these cases because the government wasn't taking a chunk of land for its own purposes but was "simply" limiting what property owners could do with their property. All sorts of regulations—zoning rules for land, rules saying that dangerous drugs can't be sold directly to the public without prescriptions—limit what a property owner can do with her property. It was hard to describe regulations limiting the use of property as a taking requiring compensation.

The Origin of the Regulatory Takings Doctrine

Hard, but not impossible. Rattling around in constitutional doctrine since at least the 1920s was the idea of a regulatory taking. Justice Oliver Wendell Holmes articulated the doctrine most clearly in a 1922 case. Pennsylvania had a statute aimed at protecting homes from collapsing when underground coal mines ate away at the ground supporting the houses. The statute said that mineowners who bought the right to mine under a person's property, a sub-surface right, had to ensure that the mining operation didn't undermine (literally) the house's foundation, even if the homeowner had not written such a provision into the contract giving the mineowner a right to work the veins beneath the surface. Pennsylvania mineowners claimed that this statute took away the property right, the right to mine, they had acquired when they bought the sub-surface right without limitation. The Supreme Court agreed.

It conceded that the government's police power gave it the ability to impose regulations to serve the public interest in safety and security and that the Pennsylvania statute, aimed at keeping houses from collapsing, did serve that interest. But, Holmes wrote, some regulations could be takings requiring compensation if they "go too far." ...

From the 1940s through the 1970s the justices didn't take the idea that a regulation could "go too far" at all seriously, rejecting challenges that looked a lot like the one the Court accepted in the coal case. Indeed, in 1987 the Court upheld a newer Pennsylvania statute that accomplished pretty much the same thing that the earlier one had tried to do.

Still, the earlier coal mining case did make it clear that regulations could be takings, and that is all that real estate developers and business interests needed to mount their challenges to modern regulations.

Regulatory Taking Was Not the Original Intent

Ironically, the idea of regulatory takings has no foundation whatever in the original meaning of the takings clause. Legal scholars have established that the drafters and ratifiers of the takings clause in the eighteenth century were worried only about the permanent physical occupations of land covered by the traditional idea of eminent domain. They knew that regulations could sometimes severely limit the value of someone's property but they clearly understood as well that the takings clause wouldn't apply to such regulations. The framers, and several generations of their successors, believed that the takings clause was entirely irrelevant when the government exercised its police powers over health, safety, and morals.

Even Justice [Antonin] Scalia, an enthusiastic proponent of the regulatory takings doctrine, agreed with this originalist view of the takings clause. Buried in a footnote in one of his takings cases is an acknowledgment that the takings clause, as originally understood, didn't apply to regulatory takings. But, Scalia wrote, the understanding as of 1791 didn't matter when the Court dealt with *state* regulations. The takings clause is in the Fifth Amendment, part of the Bill of Rights adopted in 1791. According to well-established constitutional doctrine, the Bill of Rights imposes limits only on the national government. State governments have to comply with the Constitution, of course, but the reason they do is the Fourteenth Amendment, adopted in 1868. And, Scalia said, by 1868 the idea that a regulation could be a taking was well embedded in constitutional understandings. . . .

Zoning and Environmental Regulations

For several generations, though, the Supreme Court always found that challenged regulations didn't go far enough to become takings. The Court's most important decisions involved zoning. Traditionally governments could exclude businesses from some areas if they were what lawyers called public nuisances, which were often described as businesses that were entirely legal if conducted in an appropriate area but became nuisances in the wrong place. As Supreme Court Justice George Sutherland put it in 1926, "A nuisance may be merely a right thing in a wrong place, like a pig in a parlor instead of the barnyard." Most zoning could be said to involve things similar to such nuisances, limiting housing to some areas, businesses to others, restricting the sizes of lots in one area and requiring large lots in others, and the like. The Supreme Court upheld modern zoning in a decision only four years after the Pennsylvania coal case. Zoning, it seems, was a police power regulation that didn't go too far.

Or at least traditional zoning didn't go too far. Real estate developers sometimes found traditional zoning economically beneficial to their projects, and sometimes they simply adapted to zoning requirements. The rise of middle-class social movements concerned about preserving the legacies of the past—

both in the natural environment and in human constructions—changed the economic picture for developers. Historic preservation laws sometimes posed severe obstacles to development; if a developer couldn't tear down a historic building, it might be nearly impossible to build the project the developer wanted. Some environmental regulations had almost the same effect. Laws aiming at the preservation of beaches from erosion or of wetlands from destruction sometimes made it impossible to build anything on a beachfront or on wetlands. Developers might be able to comply with other environmental regulations, but, only by eating into their profits.

The Penn Central Case

The Supreme Court first confronted challenges to modern zoning regulations in a case involving New York's Grand Central Terminal. The city adopted a historic preservation law in 1965. Like many such laws, it created a commission to designate particular buildings and districts as historical landmarks. The owners of landmark buildings have to keep their exteriors in good repair and can change the exterior appearance only with the commission's permission.

New York made the facade of Grand Central Terminal a historic landmark. Facing economic difficulties, the terminal's owner, the Penn Central Railroad, wanted to generate income by building an office on top of the terminal. New York's commission refused to allow the construction, saying that putting a fifty-five-story office tower "above a flamboyant Beaux-Arts façade seems nothing more than an aesthetic joke." Penn Central said that the landmarking amounted to a taking of its property right to develop its own land. The question for the Supreme Court was whether the historic preservation law went too far.

Rehnquist said that it did. Historic preservation laws, he wrote, were different from the traditional zoning laws the courts had upheld against takings clause challenges. Those laws, he said, simultaneously decreased the value of a particular piece of property by limiting its use and increased the value of that same piece of property by ensuring that a neighborhood as a whole would be residential or commercial. Historic preservation laws, though, singled out a few buildings to benefit the entire city but didn't give the building owners anything in return.

A Balancing Test

But Rehnquist was writing a dissent. Justice [William] Brennan wrote a majority opinion that upheld New York's historic preservation law but opened the way for continuing challenges to modern environmental and other regulations. He rejected a lot of Penn Central's challenges but did take seriously the possibility that a land use regulation could go too far. He developed a balancing test for deciding when it did: The courts had to examine the economic impact of the regulation on the property owner, particularly its impact on investment-backed expectations—in effect, not on what the owner hoped to do if things turned out right but on what the owner had already put up some money for, either in the price paid for the property or in other investments anticipating development. They also had to examine the "character" of the government's action. The more the regulation looked like a traditional exercise of the police power, the less likely it was to be a taking.

Applying this test, Brennan upheld the landmarking. It wasn't enough that landmarking reduced Grand Central Terminal's economic value to its owner. Penn Central could still use the terminal as it had for more than sixty years and would continue to get what it had expected to be a reasonable return from using the terminal as a terminal rather than as the site for an office building.

Brennan's opinion was strategically designed to hold the votes of the more conservative justices Lewis Powell and Potter Stewart. . . . Early in the opinion, Brennan stuck in a footnote saying explicitly that "we do not embrace the proposition that a 'taking' can never occur unless government has transferred physical control over a portion of a parcel." This divided the world of takings into two areas: One involved permanent physical occupations—the classical uses of eminent domain—and the other involved regulations that went too far.

Brennan certainly hoped that his multipart test for determining when a regulation went too far would lead courts to invalidate few regulations indeed. And so it has. Yet the test Brennan wrote did give real estate developers and other businesses the opportunity to increase the costs of *attempting* to regulate. They could deploy his test against any regulations they found burdensome. They might not win, but they could make it expensive for governments to try to regulate them.

The Takings Project

The Grand Central case didn't get to the Supreme Court simply because a particular individual or corporation had a lot at stake. [It was], instead, part of what two liberal critics called the Takings Project. Brennan in the Grand Central Terminal case beat back the first assault on regulatory takings, but to salvage a victory, he had to concede that sometimes regulations could amount to takings. This gave more conservative justices their chance. They argued that regulations went "too far" when they deprived landowners of the right to *any* economically beneficial uses of their property.

Grand Central Terminal of course was economically viable even after its designation as a historic landmark. Environmental regulations were sometimes a different matter. Preserving wetlands might mean keeping marshes from any development, even in areas with expanding populations. Regulations might indeed deprive the wetlands' owner of any economically viable use of the land.

The Lucas Case

The Court used a beach erosion case to announce that finally it had discovered a regulation that deprived the landowner of any economically viable use of his property. David Lucas, a burly, full-bearded developer and building contractor, was a conservative Republican activist in South Carolina politics. He was involved with some of the state's major developers and Republicans in the Wild Dunes development project on the Isle of Palms, a barrier island east of Charleston, South Carolina. The Isle of Palms is a millionaires' retreat. In 1986 Lucas paid $975,000 for two lots in Wild Dunes, where he planned to build one house for his family and another for resale. Lucas's houses would fill in some blank spaces on the map; there were houses on nearly all the nearby lots, including one on the lot between the two Lucas bought.

There was a problem, though. The Atlantic Ocean tides regularly changed the contours of the Isle of Palms, eating away at some beaches and expanding others. In 1988 South Carolina adopted a beachfront management act prohibiting development in many parts of the Isle of Palms, including on Lucas's two lots, to protect against damage to the beaches resulting from houses in areas where the tides were eroding the island. Lucas sued, claiming that the regulation barring development amounted to a taking because it deprived him of the land's entire economic value. After losing in the South Carolina Supreme Court, Lucas contacted the Pacific Legal Foundation, which offered to take his case to the U.S. Supreme Court. Lucas decided to use some South Carolina attorneys, although they welcomed the support the participants in the Takings Project offered in amicus briefs.

Scalia's Opinion

Scalia, writing for the Court's five conservatives, agreed with Lucas's argument. Quoting a medieval British author, Scalia wrote, "For what is the land but the profits thereof?" Taking all the value of property away from the owner is "the equivalent of a physical appropriation." When the government does so, it's hard to see how it's simply "adjusting the benefits and burdens of economic life," a phrase Scalia took from the Grand Central Terminal case. The government defended its regulation as necessary for environmental preservation or—invoking traditional terms—as necessary to eliminate "harmful or noxious uses" of property. But, Scalia said, "confiscatory regulations" could be justified only by "the restrictions that background principles of the State's law of property and nuisance already place upon land ownership." Traditional public nuisances, like the pig in the parlor or land uses that led to flooding a neighbor's land, were one thing; the government's power to limit *them* was indeed part of the background law. Innovative regulations like the one against beachfront erosion were another thing altogether. Scalia emphasized that the owners of the lots near Lucas's had already built houses and weren't being asked to tear them down, indicating that the limitation on Lucas's rights wasn't already part of the law.

Scalia's opinion was characteristically hard-edged, looking for a rule courts could apply rather than invoking a balancing test, seeking some rule that could be applied "on an objective, value-free basis." Justice Stevens, dissenting, thought that "[a]rresting the development of the common law" was "profoundly unwise" because it ignored the fact that the "human condition is one of constant learning and evolution—both moral and practical." (Of course Scalia's entire way of thinking rejected the idea of moral evolution.) [Harry] Blackmun's dissent was even more critical of Scalia's refusal to examine "the particular circumstances of each case." For him, what mattered was simply whether the use caused harm.

The Court sent the case back to the state courts for them to decide whether building a house on Lucas's lot was barred by "background principles of nuisance and property law." They said it wasn't, giving Lucas his victory. When the case ended, South Carolina paid Lucas $850,000 for his land and another $725,000 in interest and attorneys' fees. . . .

The Palazzolo Case

The decisive case [for The Takings Project] came from Westerly, Rhode Island, which had become a major summer resort area for the Northeast. Atlantic Avenue provides access to Westerly's main beach area. The street is something of a commercial strip at its western end, but it becomes more residential toward the east. Anthony Palazzolo, the son of Sicilian immigrants and the owner of a junkyard, ended up owning a large parcel of land near the eastern end of Atlantic Avenue, which he wanted to develop as an investment for his six children. How he got the property is a complex story, with some bearing on the outcome. The land started out as an eighteen-acre tract. It was divided into three parcels in 1939. All three were sold in 1949 to Natale and Elizabeth Urso. Ten years later the Ursos proposed to develop the land into eighty lots, and the city's zoning board approved. Palazzolo joined the Ursos in the project, setting up a corporation to develop the land. The Ursos then sold their shares to Palazzolo, who ended up owning sixty-nine lots.

Most of Palazzolo's land was wetlands, but in the 1960s Rhode Island had no wetlands regulations, and indeed, one observer wrote, "everyone was filling and dredging back then." In 1962 Palazzolo applied for a permit to dredge part of the wetlands and use the material to fill the marsh and make it useful for development. (It turned out that Rhode Island law in 1962 might not have required Palazzolo to get a permit at all. The litigation that followed might have been avoided if he had simply dredged the pond and waited to see if anyone sued him.) The state returned the application to him for more detail. He provided it, explaining that he wanted to fill the entire eighteen acres. A year later Rhode Island adopted a modest wetlands protection law. In 1966 Palazzolo applied again for approval to dredge the pond and fill the marsh for "a recreational beach facility." In April 1971 the state's regulators approved the plan, as well as an earlier plan to fill in the marsh, giving Palazzolo the choice of projects. The regulators thought again and revoked the permit in November.

Palazzolo put his project on hold. Meanwhile Rhode Island's environmentalists continued their efforts to regulate wetlands. In 1971 the state created a Coastal Resources Management Council, which adopted regulations in 1977 that prohibited filling coastal wetlands like Palazzolo's without special permission. In 1978 the corporation Palazzolo had set up was shut down by the state for failing to pay corporate income taxes. Its property was transferred automatically to Palazzolo himself. In the 1980s land prices in Westerly soared, and Palazzolo renewed his efforts to develop the land, so that, he said, he could pay college tuitions for his children. He submitted new applications to develop his land, which the regulators rejected because they were "vague and inadequate for a project of this size and nature." In the end he came up with a proposal for a beachfront facility on eleven acres of the property, with room for "fifty cars with boat trailers, a dumpster, picnic table, and barbecue pits." The Supreme Court observed acerbically that "the details do not tend to inspire the reader with an idyllic coastal image," although Palazzolo responded that the whole area was heavily developed, with vacation homes and a public beach with parking spaces for nearly three thousand cars nearby.

Palazzolo sued after the state denied this application. . . .

The Decision

The Rhode Island Supreme Court ruled against Palazzolo, using a theory that would have been a major victory for environmentalists. It said that he got the property *after* the state had adopted its comprehensive wetlands regulations, so he couldn't have expected to use the property for development.

In the language of the Lucas case, state regulations in existence when someone bought land were background rules of state law. As [Justice Anthony] Kennedy put the argument, "by prospective legislation the State can shape and define property rights and reasonable investment backed expectations." Later purchasers can't complain because they got the property knowing of the limitations the state imposed on its use.

The Supreme Court rejected that theory, which environmentalists initially treated as a serious defeat. Kennedy tried to turn a phrase by writing, "The State may not put so potent a Hobbesian stick into the Lockean bundle." An owner's notice that the state had the right to regulate couldn't by itself defeat a takings claim because that rule would allow the state "to defend any action restricting land use, no matter how extreme or unreasonable." Fair enough. But remember, the Grand Central Terminal case said that one element of the test for determining whether something was a regulatory taking was how much the regulation affected investment-backed expectations. Exactly what could a property owner expect to do with land that an existing regulation said he couldn't develop?

Kennedy didn't say anything about that question, but [Justice Sandra Day] O'Connor and Scalia did. For O'Connor, the regulations in place "help . . . shape the reasonableness" of the expectations. They should "inform the analysis." Otherwise, someone who bought property could unfairly "reap windfalls" by getting compensated for being unable to do something she should have known she couldn't do. Scalia responded by sniping at O'Connor for articulating an unintelligible approach. The windfalls she criticized were, he said, "not much different from the windfalls that occur every day at stock exchanges or antique auctions, where the knowledgeable (or the venturesome) profit at the expense of the ignorant (or the risk averse)." Maybe there was something unfair when a sharp buyer got land at a bargain price from a seller, then turned around and got more money from the government because the regulations went too far. That, though, was an unfairness between the buyer and the seller. For Scalia, "there is nothing to be said" for giving the windfall to the government—that is, "giving the malefactor the benefit of its malefaction." He proposed a simple rule: The existence of regulations was entirely irrelevant to determining whether a taking occurred.

The stakes here were fairly large. Scalia's approach would have allowed many more successful challenges to regulatory takings than O'Connor's. More important, O'Connor explicitly argued that the test for a taking could not "be reduced to any 'set formula.'" That type of approach, an all-things-considered balancing test, was the kind of test that set Scalia's teeth on edge. O'Connor's balancing test made it easier for regulators to defeat challenges to their actions. As one environmental lawyer put it, her approach "likely means that most long-established environmental and land use regulations will be largely immune from takings challenges. And they should become increasingly immune from challenge as properties change hands and additional time passes." . . .

In the end the Palazzolo case only *looked* like a defeat for environmentalists and regulators. Four justices dissented, and they certainly would choose O'Connor's approach—more generous to regulators—over Scalia's. The Court had rejected the approach most favorable to regulators, but O'Connor's wasn't all that bad from their point of view, although it certainly was confusing. It's not at all clear how you can take the existence of a regulation barring development into account without making it dispositive on the question of whether the regulation affected investment-backed expectations. Still, regulators could live with O'Connor's approach. It could mean that only "rare and unusual" regulations go too far. . . .

The End of An Era

At the end of the Rehnquist era, what had the Takings Project accomplished? On the surface, not much. The Rehnquist Court didn't force governments to pay substantially for any modern environmental, wetlands, or historic preservation regulations—if the governments proceeded carefully enough. However, the qualification is important. Before the Rehnquist Court got hold of the takings clause, environmentalists thought all they had to do was persuade legislatures to adopt regulations they liked. Today, though, businesses and developers can credibly threaten to tie regulation up in court with takings clause challenges unless the regulations are to their liking. The cases indicate that the challenges are almost always going to lose, but defending against them costs money that cities and states don't have. The Takings Project may have failed to wipe regulations off the board, but it succeeded in limiting the reach of regulations by increasing the costs of adopting them. And of course the point of the takings clause itself is to increase costs by making governments pay. So, paradoxically, what looks like the failure of the Takings Project might actually be its success.

Granting Public Access to Private Property Is a "Taking"

Antonin Scalia

The Supreme Court case Nollan v. California Coastal Commission *(1987) involved what is termed an* exaction—*a way to make a private landowner fund at least part of the costs of public improvements. The exaction in* Nollan *was the California Coastal Commission's requirement that James and Marilyn Nollan grant an easement (a zone for public access) before they would be given a permit to construct a home on their beachfront property. The easement was to run parallel to the ocean and allow the public to walk the entire distance along the coast between two public beaches that lay on either side of the Nollans' property.*

The Court ruled that requiring such an easement is a taking under the Fifth Amendment, requiring the government to compensate the property owners. In the following excerpt from the opinion, Justice Antonin Scalia rejects the coastal commission's contention that the easement requirement is merely a land-use regulation rather than a taking. He concedes that the government can impose land-use regulations that economically impact property owners without compensating them. However, such regulations must serve a "legitimate state interest." He concludes that the coastal commission has failed to demonstrate such an interest in this case, so the easement requirement is unconstitutional.

An appointee of President Ronald Reagan, Justice Antonin Scalia is commonly thought of as an extremely conservative judge. He is a strict constructionist, a legal scholar who believes the Constitution should be interpreted and applied as literally intended by its authors and not modified to reflect changing so-

Antonin Scalia, Supreme Court decision in *Nollan v. California Coastal Commission,* 483 U.S. 825, 1987.

cial or political developments. He is perhaps best known for his hard-line stances, particularly in his often biting and confrontational dissents.

The Nollans own a beachfront lot in Ventura County, California. A quarter-mile north of their property is Faria County Park, an oceanside public park with a public beach and recreation area. Another public beach area, known locally as "the Cove," lies 1,800 feet south of their lot. A concrete seawall approximately eight feet high separates the beach portion of the Nollans' property from the rest of the lot. The historic mean high tide line determines the lot's oceanside boundary.

The Nollans originally leased their property with an option to buy. The building on the lot was a small bungalow, totaling 504 square feet, which for a time they rented to summer vacationers. After years of rental use, however, the building had fallen into disrepair, and could no longer be rented out.

The Nollans' option to purchase was conditioned on their promise to demolish the bungalow and replace it. In order to do so, under [California law], they were required to obtain a coastal development permit from the California Coastal Commission. On February 25, 1982, they submitted a permit application to the Commission in which they proposed to demolish the existing structure and replace it with a three-bedroom house in keeping with the rest of the neighborhood.

The Nollans were informed that their application had been placed on the administrative calendar, and that the Commission staff had recommended that the permit be granted subject to the condition that they allow the public an easement to pass across a portion of their property bounded by the mean high tide line on one side, and their seawall on the other side. This would make it easier for the public to get to Faria County Park and the Cove. The Nollans protested imposition of the condition, but the Commission overruled their objections and granted the permit subject to their recordation of a deed restriction granting the easement. . . .

An Easement Would Be a Taking

Had California simply required the Nollans to make an easement across their beachfront available to the public on a permanent basis in order to increase public access to the beach, rather than conditioning their permit to rebuild their house on their agreeing to do so, we have no doubt there would have been a taking. To say that the appropriation of a public easement across a landowner's premises does not constitute the taking of a property interest but rather (as Justice [William] Brennan contends [in his dissent]) "a mere restriction on its use," is to use words in a manner that deprives them of all their ordinary meaning. Indeed, one of the principal uses of the eminent domain power is to assure that the government be able to require conveyance of just such interests, so long as it pays for them. Perhaps because the point is so obvious, we have never been confronted with a controversy that required us to rule upon it, but our cases' analysis of the effect of other governmental action leads to the same conclusion. We have repeatedly held that, as to property reserved by its owner for private use, "the right to exclude [others is] 'one of the most essential sticks in the bundle of rights that are commonly characterized as property.'" *Loretto v. Teleprompter Manhattan CATV Corp.* (1982), quoting *Kaiser Aetna v. United States* (1979). In *Loretto* we observed that where governmental action results in "[a] permanent physical occupation" of the property, by the government itself or by others, "our cases uniformly have found a taking to the extent of the occupation, without regard to whether the action achieves an important public benefit or has only minimal economic impact on the owner." We think a "permanent physical occupation" has occurred, for purposes of that rule, where individuals are given a permanent and continuous right to pass to and fro, so that the real property may continuously be traversed, even though no particular individual is permitted to station himself permanently upon the premises. . . .

The Permit Condition Is Also a Taking

Given, then, that requiring uncompensated conveyance of the easement outright would violate the Fourteenth Amendment, the question becomes whether requiring it to be conveyed as a condition for issuing a land-use permit alters the outcome. We have long recognized that land-use regulation does not effect a taking if it "substantially advance[s] legitimate state interests" and does not "den[y] an owner economically viable use of his land," *Agins v. Tiburon* (1980). Our cases have not elaborated on the standards for determining what constitutes a "legitimate state interest" or what type of connection between the regulation and the state interest satisfies the requirement that the former "substantially advance" the latter. They have made clear, however, that a broad range of governmental purposes and regulations satisfies these requirements. The Commission argues that among these permissible purposes are protecting the public's ability to see the beach assisting the public in overcoming the "phychological barrier" to using the beach created by a developed shorefront, and preventing congestion on the public beaches. We assume, without deciding, that this is so—in which case the Commission unquestionably would be able to deny the Nollans their permit outright if their new house (alone, or by reason of the cumulative impact produced in conjunction with other construction) would substantially impede these purposes, unless the denial would interfere so drastically with the Nollans' use of their property as to constitute a taking.

The Commission argues that a permit condition that serves the same legitimate police-power purpose as a refusal to issue the permit should not be found to be a taking if the refusal to issue the permit would not constitute a taking. We agree.

Thus, if the Commission attached to the permit some condition that would have protected the public's ability to see the beach notwithstanding construction of the new house—for example, a height limitation, a width restriction, or a ban on fences—so long as the Commission could have exercised its police power (as we have assumed it could) to forbid construction of the house altogether, imposition of the condition would also be constitutional. Moreover (and here we come closer to the facts of the present case), the condition would be constitutional even if it consisted of the requirement that the Nollans provide a viewing spot on their property for passersby with whose sighting of the ocean their new house would interfere. Although such a requirement, constituting a permanent grant of continuous access to the property, would have to be considered a taking if it were not attached to a development permit, the Commission's assumed power to forbid construction of the house in order to protect the public's view of the beach must surely include the power to condition construction upon some concession by the owner, even a concession of property rights, that serves the same end. If a prohibition designed to accomplish that purpose would be a legitimate exercise of the police power rather than a taking, it would be strange to conclude that providing the owner an alternative to that prohibition which accomplishes the same purpose is not.

Not a Valid Regulation

The evident constitutional propriety disappears, however, if the condition substituted for the prohibition utterly fails to further the end advanced as the justification for the prohibition. When that essential nexus is eliminated, the situation becomes the same as if California law forbade shouting fire in a crowded theater, but granted dispensations to those willing to contribute $100 to the state treasury. While a ban on shouting fire can be a core exercise of the State's police power to protect the public safety, and can thus meet even our stringent standards for regulation of speech, adding the unrelated condition alters the purpose to one which, while it may be legitimate, is inadequate to sustain the ban. Therefore, even though, in a sense, requiring a $100 tax contribution in order to shout fire is a lesser restriction on speech than an outright ban, it would not pass constitutional muster. Similarly here, the lack of nexus between the condition and the original purpose of the building restriction converts that purpose to something other than what it was. The purpose then becomes, quite simply, the obtaining of an easement to serve some valid governmental purpose, but without payment of compensation. Whatever may be the outer limits of "legitimate state interests" in the takings and land-use context, this is not one of them. In short, unless the permit condition serves the same governmental purpose as the development ban, the building restriction is not a valid regulation of land use but "an out-and-out plan of extortion." *J. E. D. Associates, Inc. v. Atkinson* (1981).

The "Access" Argument Fails

The Commission claims that it concedes as much, and that we may sustain the condition at issue here by finding that it is reasonably related to the public need or burden that the Nollans' new house creates or to which it contributes. We can accept, for purposes of discussion, the Commission's proposed test as to how close a "fit" between the condition and the burden is required, because we find that this case does not meet even the most untailored standards. The Commission's principal contention to the contrary essentially turns on a play on the word "access." The Nollans' new house, the Commission found, will interfere with "visual access" to the beach. That in turn (along with other shorefront development) will interfere with the desire of people who drive past the Nollans' house to use the beach, thus creating a "psychological barrier" to "access." The Nollans' new house will also, by a process not altogether clear from the Commission's opinion but presumably potent enough to more than offset the effects of the psychological barrier, increase the use of the public beaches, thus creating the need for more "access." These burdens on "access" would be alleviated by a requirement that the Nollans provide "lateral access" to the beach.

Rewriting the argument to eliminate the play on words makes clear that there is nothing to it. It is quite impossible to understand how a requirement that people already on the public beaches be able to walk across the Nollans' property reduces any obstacles to viewing the beach created by the new house. It is also impossible to understand how it lowers any "psychological barrier" to using the public beaches, or how it helps to remedy any additional congestion on them caused by construction of the Nollans' new house. We therefore find that the Commission's imposition of the permit condition cannot be treated as an exercise of its land-use power for any of these purposes. Our conclusion on this point is consistent with the approach taken by every other court that has considered the question, with the exception of the California state courts.

Justice Brennan argues that imposition of the access requirement is not irrational. In his version of the Commission's argument, the reason for the requirement is that in its absence, a person looking toward the beach from the road will see a street of residential structures including the Nollans' new home and conclude that there is no public beach nearby. If, however, that person sees people passing and repassing along the dry sand behind the Nollans' home, he will realize that there is a public beach somewhere in the vicinity. The Commission's action, however, was based on the opposite factual finding that the wall of houses completely blocked the view of the beach and that a person looking from the road would not be able to see it at all.

A "Comprehensive Program" Requires Compensation

Even if the Commission had made the finding that Justice Brennan proposes, however, it is not certain that it would suffice. We do not share Justice Brennan's confidence that the Commission "should have little difficulty in the future in utilizing its expertise to demonstrate a specific connection between provisions for access and burdens on access" that will avoid the effect of today's decision. We view the Fifth Amendment's Property Clause to be more than a pleading requirement, and compliance with it to be more than an exercise in cleverness and imagination. As indicated earlier, our cases describe the condition for abridgment of property rights through the police power as a "substantial advanc[ing]" of a legitimate state interest. We are inclined to be particularly careful about the adjective where the actual conveyance of property is made a condition to the lifting of a land-use restriction, since in that context there is heightened risk that the purpose is avoidance of the compensation requirement, rather than the stated police-power objective.

We are left, then, with the Commission's justification for the access requirement unrelated to land-use regulation:

> "Finally, the Commission notes that there are several existing provisions of pass and repass lateral access benefits already given by past Faria Beach Tract applicants as a result of prior coastal permit decisions. The access required as a condition of this permit is part of a comprehensive program to provide continuous public access along Faria Beach as the lots undergo development or redevelopment."

That is simply an expression of the Commission's belief that the public interest will be served by a continuous strip of publicly accessible beach along the coast. The Commission may well be right that it is a good idea, but that does not establish that the Nollans (and other coastal residents) alone can be compelled to contribute to its realization. Rather, California is free to advance its "comprehensive program," if it wishes, by using its power of eminent domain for this "public purpose"; but if it wants an easement across the Nollans' property, it must pay for it.

A Lengthy Moratorium on Development Is a "Taking"

William H. Rehnquist

The Supreme Court case Tahoe-Sierra Preservation Council, Inc. v. Tahoe Regional Planning Agency *(2002) involved a moratorium on all development in an area on Lake Tahoe, a pristine mountain lake on the California-Nevada border. The moratorium was put in place for a thirty-two month period from 1981 to 1983 while environmentally sound development plans were drafted. Various property owners sued on the grounds that the moratorium constituted a taking of their property as defined by the Fifth Amendment. The Supreme Court ruled that because the moratorium was a temporary measure, it was merely a regulation of land use, not an outright physical taking.*

The following excerpt is from a dissent in the Tahoe-Sierra *case by former Chief Justice William H. Rehnquist. Rehnquist argued that the moratorium was a taking because it deprived the property owners of "all economically beneficial uses" of their property. Moreover, he rejected the notion that a thirty-two month moratorium on development could be defined as temporary. In fact, due to subsequent government actions, the ban on building actually lasted six years. For these reasons, Rehnquist found that the land-use regulation at issue was not mere regulation—it was the same as a physical taking of the property. Therefore, he concluded, the owners of the property should be compensated.*

William H. Rehnquist sat on the U.S. Supreme Court for more than thirty-three years—nearly twenty of them as Chief Justice. In his early years on the Court, Rehnquist was often the lone dissenter in the company of many liberal colleagues. As Chief Justice, however, he presided as the Court took a turn in a

William H. Rehnquist, Supreme Court decision in *Tahoe-Sierra Preservation Council, Inc., v. Tahoe Regional Planning Agency*, 535 U.S. 302, 2002.

more conservative direction. Rehnquist served as the Chief Justice until his death in September 2005.

For over half a decade petitioners were prohibited from building homes, or any other structures, on their land. Because the Takings Clause requires the government to pay compensation when it deprives owners of all economically viable use of their land, and because a ban on all development lasting almost six years does not resemble any traditional land-use planning device, I dissent. . . .

Lucas [*v. South Carolina Coastal Council* (1992)] reaffirmed our "frequently expressed" view that "when the owner of real property has been called upon to sacrifice *all* economically beneficial uses in the name of the common good, that is, to leave his property economically idle, he has suffered a taking." The District Court in this case held that the ordinances and resolutions in effect between August 24, 1981, and April 25, 1984, "did in fact deny the plaintiffs all economically viable use of their land." The Court of Appeals did not overturn this finding. And the 1984 injunction, issued because the environmental thresholds issued by respondent did not permit the development of single-family residences, forced petitioners to leave their land economically idle for at least another three years. The Court does not dispute that petitioners were forced to leave their land economically idle during this period. But the Court refuses to apply *Lucas* on the ground that the deprivation was "temporary."

No Temporary Versus Permanent Distinction

Neither the Takings Clause nor our case law supports such a distinction. For one thing, a distinction between "temporary" and "permanent" prohibitions is tenuous. The "temporary" prohibition in this case that the Court finds is not a taking lasted almost six years. The "permanent" prohibition that the

Court held to be a taking in *Lucas* lasted less than two years. The "permanent" prohibition in *Lucas* lasted less than two years because the law, as it often does, changed. The South Carolina Legislature in 1990 decided to amend the 1988 Beachfront Management Act to allow the issuance of "'special permits' for the construction or reconstruction of habitable structures seaward of the baseline." Land-use regulations are not irrevocable. . . . Under the Court's decision today, the takings question turns entirely on the initial label given a regulation, a label that is often without much meaning. There is every incentive for government to simply label any prohibition on development "temporary," or to fix a set number of years. As in this case, this initial designation does not preclude the government from repeatedly extending the "temporary" prohibition into a long-term ban on all development. The Court now holds that such a designation by the government is conclusive even though in fact the moratorium greatly exceeds the time initially specified. Apparently, the Court would not view even a 10-year moratorium as a taking under *Lucas* because the moratorium is not "permanent."

Our opinion in *First English Evangelical Lutheran Church of Glendale v. County of Los Angeles* (1987) rejects any distinction between temporary and permanent takings when a landowner is deprived of all economically beneficial use of his land. *First English* stated that "'temporary takings which, as here, deny a landowner all use of his property, are not different in kind from permanent takings, for which the Constitution clearly requires compensation." Because of *First English*'s rule that "temporary deprivations of use are compensable under the Takings Clause," the Court in *Lucas* found nothing problematic about the later developments that potentially made the ban on development temporary.

More fundamentally, even if a practical distinction between temporary and permanent deprivations were plausible, to treat the two differently in terms of takings law would be at odds with the justification for the *Lucas* rule. The *Lucas* rule is derived from the fact that a "total deprivation of use is, from the landowner's point of view, the equivalent of a physical appropriation." The regulation in *Lucas* was the "practical equivalence" of a long-term physical appropriation, *i.e.*, a condemnation, so the Fifth Amendment required compensation. The "practical equivalence," from the landowner's point of view, of a "temporary" ban on all economic use is a forced leasehold. For example, assume the following situation: Respondent is contemplating the creation of a National Park around Lake Tahoe to preserve its scenic beauty. Respondent decides to take a 6-year leasehold over petitioners' property, during which any human activity on the land would be prohibited, in order to prevent any further destruction to the area while it was deciding whether to request that the area be designated a National Park.

Surely that leasehold would require compensation. In a series of World War II-era cases in which the Government had condemned leasehold interests in order to support the war effort, the Government conceded that it was required to pay compensation for the leasehold interest. From petitioners' standpoint, what happened in this case is no different than if the government had taken a 6-year lease of their property. The Court ignores this "practical equivalence" between respondent's deprivation and the deprivation resulting from a leasehold. In so doing, [in the dissenting words of Circuit Court Judge Alex Kozinski in the case below] the Court allows the government to "do by regulation what it cannot do through eminent domain—i.e., take private property without paying for it."

No Regulation Versus Physical Taking Distinction

Instead of acknowledging the "practical equivalence" of this case and a condemned leasehold, the Court analogizes to other areas of takings law in which we have distinguished between regulations and physical appropriations. But whatever basis there is for such distinctions in those contexts does not apply when a regulation deprives a landowner of all economically beneficial use of his land. In addition to the "practical equivalence" from the landowner's perspective of such a regulation and a physical appropriation, we have held that a regulation denying all productive use of land does not implicate the traditional justification for differentiating between regulations and physical appropriations. . . .

The Court also reads *Lucas* as being fundamentally concerned with value rather than with the denial of "all economically beneficial or productive use of land." But *Lucas* repeatedly discusses its holding as applying where "*no* productive or economically beneficial use of land is permitted."

Lucas is implicated when the government deprives a landowner of "all economically beneficial or productive use of land." The District Court found, and the Court agrees, that the moratorium "temporarily" deprived petitioners of "'all economically viable use of their land.'" Because the rationale for the *Lucas* rule applies just as strongly in this case, the "temporary" denial of all viable use of land for six years is a taking.

Proper Land Use Planning

The Court worries that applying *Lucas* here compels finding that an array of traditional, short-term, land-use planning devices are takings. But since the beginning of our regulatory takings jurisprudence, we have recognized that property rights "are enjoyed under an implied limitation." [*Pennsylvania Coal Co. v. Mahon* (1922).]

When a regulation merely delays a final land use decision, we have recognized that there are other background principles of state property law that prevent the delay from being deemed a taking. We thus noted in *First English* that our discussion of temporary takings did not apply "in the case of normal delays in obtaining building permits, changes in zoning ordinances, variances, and the like." We reiterated this last Term: "The right to improve property, of course, is subject to the reasonable exercise of state authority, including the enforcement of valid zoning and land-use restrictions." *Palazzolo v. Rhode Island* (2001). Zoning regulations existed as far back as colonial Boston, and New York City enacted the first comprehensive zoning ordinance in 1916. Thus, the short-term delays attendant to zoning and permit regimes are a longstanding feature of state property law and part of a landowner's reasonable investment-backed expectations.

Long-Term Moratoria Are Takings

But a moratorium prohibiting all economic use for a period of six years is not one of the longstanding, implied limitations of state property law. Moratoria are "interim controls on the use of land that seek to maintain the status quo with respect to land development in an area by either 'freezing' existing land uses or by allowing the issuance of building permits for only certain land uses that would not be inconsistent with a contemplated zoning plan or zoning change." E. Ziegler, Rathkopf's *The Law of Zoning and Planning* (2001). Typical moratoria thus prohibit only certain categories of development, such as fast-food restaurants or adult businesses or all commercial development. Such moratoria do not implicate *Lucas* because they do not deprive landowners of all economically beneficial use of their land. As for moratoria that prohibit all development, these do not have the lineage of permit and zoning requirements and thus it is less certain that property is acquired under the "implied limitation" of a moratorium prohibiting all development. Moreover, unlike a permit system in which it is expected that a project will be approved so long as certain conditions are satisfied, a moratorium that prohibits all uses is by definition contemplating a new land-use plan that would prohibit all uses.

But this case does not require us to decide as a categorical matter whether moratoria prohibiting all economic use are an implied limitation of state property law, because the duration of this "moratorium" far exceeds that of ordinary moratoria. As the Court recognizes, state statutes authorizing the issuance of moratoria often limit the moratoria's duration. California, where much of the land at issue in this case is located, provides that a moratorium "shall be of no further force and effect 45 days from its date of adoption," and caps extension of the moratorium so that the total duration cannot exceed two years. Another State [Oregon] limits moratoria to 120 days, with the possibility of a single 6-month extension. Others [Colorado and New Jersey] limit moratoria to six months without any possibility of an extension. Indeed, it has long been understood that moratoria on development exceeding these short time periods are not a legitimate planning device.

Resolution 83-21 [in this case] reflected this understanding of the limited duration of moratoria in initially limiting the moratorium in this case to 90 days. But what resulted—a "moratorium" lasting nearly six years—bears no resemblance to the short-term nature of traditional moratoria as understood from these background examples of state property law.

Because the prohibition on development of nearly six years in this case cannot be said to resemble any "implied limitation" of state property law, it is a taking that requires compensation.

The Bill of Rights

CHAPTER 4

Current Issues and Perspectives on Property Rights

Using State Law to Expand Property Rights

Jay M. Feinman

In the following selection law professor Jay M. Feinman describes the efforts of property-right proponents to change state law to their advantage. According to Feinman, these advocates are attempting to bring about laws that will establish broad definitions of what government actions constitute the taking of property justifying compensation. Some states have passed laws declaring that a certain reduction in a property's value is automatically a taking that would require compensation. One Oregon law declared that any reduction in value is automatically a taking (although that law has been deemed unconstitutional). Feinman concludes that these efforts represent a concerted program to limit the government's ability to impose regulations to protect the environment and control development.

Jay M. Feinman is a professor at Rutgers School of Law. He has authored several articles and books, including Un-Making Law: The Conservative Campaign to Roll Back the Common Law.

Takings compensation statutes in a number of states define what constitutes a taking more clearly and more severely than the courts do, and thereby attempt to increase the costs of government regulation by making many more regulations subject to a compensation requirement. The statutes set a threshold above which any reduction in value of property is automatically a taking: 20 percent of the property's value in Louisiana, 25 percent in Texas, 40 percent in Mississippi, and an "inordinate burden" on the property in Florida.

Jay M. Feinman, *Un-Making Law: The Conservative Campaign to Roll Back Common Law*. Boston: Beacon Press, 2004, pp. 141–45. Copyright © 2004 by Jay M. Feinman. All rights reserved. Reproduced by permission of Beacon Press, Boston.

Florida Law

The Florida and Texas compensation statutes are the most notable. Florida has had a strong property rights movement since the 1970s, with numerous commissions and proposals. In 1994, the movement mounted a petition drive to amend the Florida Constitution so that any government action that diminished the value of property would entitle the owner to compensation determined by a jury without requiring him to resort to administrative remedies. The conservative Florida Legal Foundation was a prime mover behind the $3 million petition drive, supported by corporations that owned huge amounts of land subject to environmental and development regulation, including the St. Joe Paper Company and the U.S. Sugar Corporation. The Florida Supreme Court struck down the proposed amendment because it did not meet constitutional requirements.

The movement in Florida gained renewed power after the 1994 elections, in which Democrat Lawton Chiles barely defeated Jeb Bush (while brother George W. was winning election as governor of Texas) and the Republicans gained control of the Senate for the first time since Reconstruction. The Florida Legal Foundation and large corporations were joined in pushing for legislation by farmers and developers who were increasingly subject to regulations designed to protect wetlands and the oceanfront. In an attempt to forestall more radical measures, Governor Chiles convened a working group to develop a compromise proposal. The group's proposal was eventually enacted, with one last-minute addition written by lobbyist Wade Hopping for large landowners and big businesses. Instead of protecting "existing uses" of property, the statute provided compensation measured against "reasonable, foreseeable, nonspeculative" uses of land, a major change that dramatically increased the compensation available to owners.

The Florida statute has chilled the adoption of some new environmental protections. Palm Beach County, for example, halted its plan to limit development of a 20,000-acre agricultural reserve near the Everglades, fearing a wave of litigation under the statute. Dade County officials refrained from extending the Ocean Beach Historic District to prevent the construction of a thirty-story condominium, under threats from the developer's attorney.

Texas Law

Texas, too, has had a longstanding, active property rights movement. In 1995, Governor George W. Bush signed legislation under which a landowner is entitled to compensation when a governmental action reduces the value of the owner's property by 25 percent or more. This strict standard allows property rights advocates to trumpet the statute as a model. As elsewhere, though, without a public reporting requirement for agencies or reported cases applying the statute, its effects are hard to measure. The statute itself contains many exclusions, leaving outside its scope actions taken to fulfill an obligation mandated by state or federal law such as environmental and coastal zone protections, regulation of nuisances, and a variety of special-interest exceptions such as certain rules about water safety, hunting, fishing, and protecting oil and gas resources and groundwater.

Public Opposition to Takings Measures

Despite the Right's claims to populism and protecting the small farmer and individual landowner, until the 2000 election, every takings provisions put to the voters had been rejected. Rhode Island voters adopted a constitutional amendment in 1986 that limits the application of takings law to prevent environmental regulation. The Washington legislature was one of the first to adopt legislation pushed by the property rights movement, enacting a takings impact assessment law in 1991 and a compensation statute in 1994, but environmentalists quickly amassed 231,000 signatures to put the issue to a referendum. Although the statute's supporters spent twice as much as its opponents, the referendum defeated the statute by a 60-40 margin. The key to the victory was the predicted expense of the measure. One study estimated its cost to the state at $11 billion, with municipalities having either to spend 10 percent of their budgets compensating landowners or to abandon land use regulations. "The thought of hard-earned taxpayer money going right into the coffers of shopping-mall developers really galled people," said Ed Zuckerman of the Washington Environmental PAC. Following the 1992 enactment of a takings law in Arizona, environmentalists gathered 71,000 signatures to put the measure to a public vote. Takings advocates raised a $600,000 war chest from real estate brokers, developers, cattle ranchers, and the mining industry, again outspending environmentalists two to one, but grassroots support for environmental protection led to the defeat of the takings measure.

Oregon's Compensation Law

Oregon's Measure 7 is the most extreme version of a compensation provision. An amendment to the Oregon constitution adopted in 2000 and struck down by the state supreme court on procedural grounds in 2002, Measure 7 would have required the payment of compensation whenever the state or local government adopted a regulation that restricted the use and thereby reduced the value of real property to any degree. Thus, a new zoning regulation that prevented the construction of a factory in a residential neighborhood, or a restriction to protect historically significant buildings, open space, or wildlife habitat would have required payment to the affected landowner, whether the reduction in value was one dollar or one million dollars, 1 percent of the value or 90 percent. Oregon attorney general Hardy Myers's opinion about the scope of the bill ruled that grocery stores that had to accept returns of recyclable bottles under the state's Bottle Bill would have a takings claim, because they had to set aside part of their store property for the storage of the bottles. A municipality could require the owner of a store or office building to provide parking spaces only by paying for the requirement. Ditto restrictions on building height to protect scenic views of Mount Hood, or a ban on the construction of cell phone transmission towers. Even the measure's sponsors admitted that it would cost the state and municipalities $5.4 billion a year.

In the November 2000 election, Measure 7, one of a stupefying twenty-six initiatives on the Oregon ballot, passed by a 53 to 47 percent margin. How did such a measure pass in tree-hugging Oregon, a state devoted to protecting salmon, wilderness, and bike trails? "This definitely slipped in under the radar," according to Randy Tucker of 1000 Friends of Oregon, a citizens' organization promoting land use planning. Opponents of the measure, from the Sierra Club and the American Farmland Trust to Democratic governor John Kitzhaber, only engaged in a last-minute publicity blitz during the final week of the campaign, when polls showed a slim margin of voters favoring the measure.

The primary sponsors of Measure 7 were two conservative activist groups, Oregon Taxpayers United (OTU) and Oregonians in Action. Oregon Taxpayers United is the project of conservative tax activist and radio host Bill Sizemore. Sizemore also runs a company that promotes ballot measures for OTU and others, for a fee; aside from Measure 7, their proposals in 2000 included provisions to allow unlimited deductions for federal income taxes on state returns (thereby cutting the state's tax revenues by a billion dollars a year) and to limit union payroll deductions. After the supreme court invalidated Measure 7, its sponsors drafted a new version, Initiative 36, slated for the November 2004 ballot, which would require payment to property owners when a land use regulation restricts the use of property or reduces its value, again to any extent or in any amount. . . .

A Mixed Result

The legislative record of the property rights movement is mixed. When put to the voters in a visible and understandable way, takings compensation proposals are almost always rejected. Even in the legislatures and executive branch, the to-and-fro of interests and the practical accommodation to the work of government produces statutes or enforcements that are less sweeping than their advocates would like. These problems could be solved by making absolute property rights a constitutional requirement, so the movement has engaged in aggressive litigation campaigns to achieve that goal.

Environmental Regulations Violate Property Rights

Russ J. Harding

In the following article Russ J. Harding contends that government regulations meant to protect the environment often restrict the ways that property owners can use their land, sometimes greatly reducing the value of the property. He contends that these regulations go beyond traditional land-use requirements, such as zoning laws, and amount to "regulatory takings." Because environmental protection is in the interest of all members of society, individual property owners should not be burdened with these costs, Harding insists. Instead, government should compensate property owners for the costs of environmental preservation, just as owners are compensated for property taken through eminent domain.

Russ J. Harding is a senior environmental policy analyst at the Mackinac Center for Public Policy, a nonprofit public policy research institute in Michigan.

Many Americans are outraged by the U.S. Supreme Court decision last June [2005] that allowed the city of New London, Conn., to take the home and property of Susette Kelo to make way for a private economic development project. In this case, the power of eminent domain was not used for a public function, such as a government building, school or highway, but instead to transfer an individual's property to a private developer.

Many state legislatures, including Michigan's, are moving to pass laws to prevent the abuse of power typified in the Kelo case. The Michigan Senate has passed and sent to the House

Russ J. Harding, "A Taking By Any Other Name," Mackinac Center for Public Policy, November 28, 2005. Copyright © 2005 Mackinac Center for Public Policy. Reproduced by permission.

legislation that would provide some protections against government takings of private property for economic development.

A landowner's property should not be taken by the government for economic development purposes. But in Kelo-type cases, at least the government must monetarily compensate the landowner. Such is not the case with a "regulatory taking."

Taxing Individual Property Owners

Regulatory takings differ from physical takings in that the government does not assume possession of the property. Rather, the owner's use of the property is restricted by regulations—most commonly environmental prohibitions.

Regulatory takings of private property have become common in Michigan and throughout the country. Among the most common type of regulatory takings in Michigan is wetlands regulations enforced by the state Department of Environmental Quality. Wetlands may offer environmental benefits, such as providing wildlife habitat and improving water quality by filtering runoff near streams and lakes. However, the benefits of preserving wetlands accrue to society in general, not just the landowner whose property features wetlands. Often times, in fact, the presence of wetlands is a liability when the landowner is barred by regulation from using the property.

A regulatory taking is, in effect, a tax imposed on a single property owner. If the land is worth $200,000 before its designation as wetlands, but only $125,000 after such designation restricts use of the property, the cost of the regulation—$75,000—is borne solely by the property owner. But the cost of protecting wetlands—or any other social good—should be carried by all of society.

The Michigan Constitution provides for compensation for private property takings in Article 10, Section 2:

Private property shall not be taken for public use without just compensation therefor being first made or secured in a manner prescribed by law. Compensation shall be determined in proceedings in a court of record.

An Extreme Standard

It has been argued that some regulation of private property is permissible—such as the zoning of property as commercial or residential—and therefore does not amount to a government taking. The courts, however, have carried that rationale to an extreme, consistently ruling that in order for a taking to occur on property containing wetlands, nearly all use of the land must be lost. This extreme standard set by the courts results in the denial of compensation in most wetland cases, since parcels of property seldom contain 100 percent wetlands. Wetlands typically are interspersed with uplands. Furthermore, regulatory policy should be set by elected representatives of the people, not activist courts.

The protection of constitutional rights needs to be reintroduced to the system of regulation. If the government deems it necessary to restrict the use of private property for environmental protection (or any other reason), landowners should be compensated. It is one thing to protect wetlands on property held in public trust; it is entirely something else to require private landowners to bear those costs without compensation.

Government officials, with the assistance of judges who have shown little regard for private property rights, have been able to take private property for politically popular causes without having to pay for it. As lawmakers work to protect property owners from government takings for economic development, they would be wise to also address the widespread problem of regulatory takings.

Citizens Must Act

If the Legislature fails to protect private property, it will fall to citizens to address the issue through a ballot initiative. That is precisely what happened . . . in Oregon, where voters handily passed a ballot initiative requiring state government to pay landowners for the loss of use of their property. The Oregon law specifies that if the government cannot afford to pay the landowner, or chooses not to, then the land use restrictions do not take effect.

A lower court subsequently declared the Oregon law to be unconstitutional, and issued an injunction barring its enforcement while the case is under appeal. Nevertheless, it is past time for Michigan property owners to be afforded the protections demanded by Oregon citizens and which are among the most fundamental of our constitutional rights.

The Property Rights Movement Is Extremist

Jennifer Bradley

The property rights movement consists primarily of conservative and libertarian activists who oppose government regulation of private property. They are especially critical of environmental regulations that limit the ways property owners can use their land in order to protect endangered species, wetlands, and other sensitive ecosystems. Activists consider such regulations to be takings for which the government should provide compensation. In the following excerpt Jennifer Bradley criticizes efforts of the property rights movement. She insists that the movement is wrong to equate government regulation with the types of takings involved in eminent domain procedures. Private property has always been subject to government regulation, she notes, and such oversight is essential in order to ensure the public good.

Jennifer Bradley is an attorney at Community Rights Counsel, a public-interest law firm.

One of the most important Supreme Court rulings of the last few years was not about church-state issues, affirmative action, or even the war on terrorism. It was about real estate—15 houses located in a forlorn part of southeastern Connecticut called New London.

On its face, the case, *Kelo v. New London* . . . was a victory for New London and other flailing cities that have tried to remake tired, depleted neighborhoods into glittering urban showplaces using the power of eminent domain. *Kelo* held that local governments looking for redevelopment sites that might require condemnation could look throughout a munici-

Jennifer Bradley, "Property Wrongs: In Kelo's Wake, a Raft of Anti-Regulatory Initiatives from the Right," *American Prospect*, January 2006. Copyright 2006 The American Prospect, Inc. All rights reserved. Reproduced with permission from The American Prospect, 11 Beacon Street, Suite 1120, Boston, MA 02108.

pality, rather than restricting their search to blighted areas most likely to be inhabited by poor and minority residents. In affirming that middle-class residents, not just the poor, should share the often intensely felt costs of urban improvement, the case was actually rather progressive.

But now, several months after the June 2005 ruling, it seems clear that *Kelo* was a pyrrhic victory—for cities desperately trying to stem the tide of people, jobs, and tax dollars flowing to the suburbs, for the idea that everyone has a stake in redevelopment, and for those who believe that one of the central tasks of government is to balance individual rights with community health, safety, and prosperity. Conservative strategist Grover Norquist has deemed the Kelo decision "manna from heaven" for the property-rights movement, and predicted, "20 years from now, people will look back at Kelo the way people look back at *Roe v. Wade*," as an unpopular decision that galvanized the losing side and created a decades-long legal and cultural battle. For the property-rights movement, the *Kelo* loss could turn out to be better than a win.

The *Kelo* Decision

In 1998, when it embarked on its redevelopment plan, the tiny city of New London was dying. It lost 30 percent of its residents between 1960 and 1998. About 1,800 of the town's 23,860 remaining residents were unemployed. Federal military base closings in 1996 had taken one of the town's major employers, the Naval Undersea Warfare Center, which had once employed 1,500 people at a waterfront site in a neighborhood called Fort Trumbull. In February 1998, in the first bit of economic good news in years, the Pfizer pharmaceutical company announced it would build a new research facility next to the same neighborhood.

Over almost two years, the city explored how to build an economic revival in Fort Trumbull that would reach the rest of the city: The final redevelopment plan that the City Council approved would remake 90 acres of Fort Trumbull, and included new roads and infrastructure, a museum, a marina, and a riverwalk alongside office towers, shops, and condominiums. All told, it would bring between 1,200 and 2,300 jobs to the city. Two Connecticut courts agreed that this plan was not conceived to benefit Pfizer or any private developer. This is the public purpose that the Supreme Court upheld in *Kelo*: a redevelopment project that would create hundreds of jobs, new public amenities, and a chance for a city to reverse its long, grim decline. The decision was the latest in a long line of cases in which the court upheld the notion that government has the right, sometimes even the duty, to intervene in the economy.

Opponents of the decision have complained that *Kelo* allows cities to blithely take one person's property and transfer it to the highest bidder. That is simply false. As the court wrote in *Kelo*, "[I]t has long been accepted that the sovereign may not take the property of A for the sole purpose of transferring it to another private party B, even though A is paid just compensation. . . . [T]he City would no doubt be forbidden from taking petitioners' land for the purpose of conferring a private benefit on a particular private party." The *Kelo* case was not about a town selling out hardworking families and little old ladies to a rapacious corporation. It was about a desperate place trying to keep itself and its citizens afloat.

Backlash

Although a paper victory, *Kelo* has created a massive backlash and ultimately may be a practical defeat for many cities. Just days after the decision, the Institute for Justice, a libertarian law firm that represented Susette Kelo and her neighbors, launched a $3 million campaign to change state and local condemnation laws. In the legislative sessions . . . legislators in almost half the states will consider new laws that forbid eminent domain for the purpose of economic development. Proposed federal bills, including a Senate appropriations rider and a bill that passed the House 376 to 38, . . . would also prevent state and local officials from using federal funds for economic development projects that use eminent domain.

But the property-rights movement is not stopping at eminent domain. They want to extend the electric unpopularity of *Kelo* to cripple governments' ability to protect the environment, endangered species, the rights of neighboring landowners, and the community. Their argument is simple: There is no difference between government's condemning your property through eminent domain and government's regulating your use of your own property, for example by forbidding land owners from building on sensitive wetlands, which control floods and filter flowing water, or destroying the habitat of endangered species or the species themselves. As Bill Moshofsky, the president of Oregonians in Action, a leading property-rights group, wrote, . . . "Regulations that reduce the value of public land to provide public benefits are no different than taking private land for roads, public buildings or wildlife preserves. Yet the courts have required compensation for every foot of land taken for roads, buildings, or preserves, and no compensation for land taken by regulations."

This argument muddles two different lines of constitutional inquiry. The Constitution's fifth amendment states, "[N]or shall private property be taken for public use, without just compensation." The condemnations at issue in the *Kelo* case, like all condemnations, were clearly takings of private property and required compensation. By contrast, regulations that leave property in the hands of the owner but limit what he or she can do with it rarely constitute takings. The difference has been long recognized in American law: We have a right to own property, but not an unlimited right to do whatever we want with it. Our exercise of our property rights has a tremendous effect on our neighbors' property and their rights.

Courts recognize this complicated intertwining. The property-rights movement, by contrast, ignores it.

Attacking Environmental Regulations

The property-rights movement is already using the *Kelo* decision to frame the debate over the Endangered Species Act (ESA), arguing that changes in the law are necessary to shore up property rights under attack by the court. "Americans have clearly seen, through the recent Supreme Court ruling in *Kelo v. New London*, that local governments can now take private property for any scheme they can devise. However, the precedent for such cavalier disregard for property rights comes directly from the ESA," fumed an article by activist Tom DeWeese of the American Policy Center. Republican Congressman Richard Pombo from California has tried repeatedly since his election to Congress in 1992 to gut the act. At a rally . . . he said about *Kelo*, "This may be the court decision that makes Americans realize we are losing those rights" to private property.

A few days after the *Kelo* decision came down, a draft summary of Pombo's Endangered Species Act "reform" bill was leaked to environmental groups. The draft would have required the federal government to pay property owners when protections for endangered species would have reduced the value of a portion of their property by more than half. In other words, if an endangered toad lived on one acre of a 10-acre ranch, and the value of that single acre fell by more than 50 percent, the owner would have a claim against the federal government.

Predictably, Pombo's draft bill was savaged by environmentalists. But it was also attacked by his usual property-rights allies, furious that the compensation standards did not go far enough. One said the bill "should be renamed Kelo 2." A letter signed by 80 property-rights and conservative activists, including Paul Weyrich and Phyllis Schlafly said that with

Kelo, "Such blatant disregard for property rights and the Fifth Amendment sent shockwaves throughout the nation." The 50 percent compensation provision, they said, was "wholly insufficient" and a "weak acknowledgement of property rights."

Pombo apparently was swayed. The final version of the Threatened and Endangered Species Recovery Act (TESRA) enables an owner to receive 100 percent of the fair market value of "foregone uses" of her property that would harm endangered species. This is an invitation for unscrupulous landowners to file specious claims. They might build a shopping mall, for example, but are forbidden from doing so by the Endangered Species Act, and force the government to pay up. The bill flew from introduction to passage by a 229 to 193 vote in the House in just 10 days. . . .

You can expect more of these post-*Kelo* efforts going forward. By likening regulations that protect the environment, the rights of other landowners, and the community to the unpopular *Kelo* condemnations, property-rights extremists intend to continue their decades-long project of delegitimizing government regulation of property. Progressives can, and do, disagree about the merits of New London's project. But they should be clear that the *Kelo* case is being used to fuel a fight not over eminent domain, but over the legitimacy of government's ability to do what it has always done—balance the rights of individuals with the communal good.

The Power of Eminent Domain Is Being Abused

George F. Will

In the following excerpt syndicated columnist George F. Will argues that local and state governments nationwide are abusing the power of eminent domain in order to seize property. Eminent domain has traditionally been used when land is needed for public use, such as the construction of roads and public buildings. However, rather than only taking property for a genuine public use, as required by the Constitution, state and local governments now seize property in order to sell it to developers, thereby enriching speculators and increasing tax revenues while leaving citizens deprived of their family homes. Will characterizes this process as "theft by government" and calls for new laws to prevent the practice.

Norwood, Ohio—in this town, which is surrounded by Cincinnati, there is a field surrounded by a high chain-link fence. Across a street on one side of the field is a residential neighborhood of modest homes. On another side is an upscale shopping center with a Starbucks, and Birkenstock and Smith & Hawken stores. The field used to be a neighborhood with 99 houses and small businesses, but almost all the structures have been destroyed. One of the homes that remain—the developer of the shopping center wants to level all so he can expand his domain—was for 35 years the first and only home owned by Carl and Joy Gamble, who are both in their mid-60s.

Now they live across the Ohio River in Kentucky, in the basement of their daughter's house, as they wait for the Ohio Supreme Court to decide their home's fate. Norwood's gov-

George F. Will, "Legal Theft in Norwood," *Newsweek*, April 24, 2006, p. 94. Copyright © 2006 Newsweek, Inc. Reproduced by permission of the author.

ernment seized it to enrich itself by enriching a taxpaying developer who has a $125 million project.

The Gambles say that when the city offered them money for their house, they were not interested. "We had everything we wanted, right there," says Joy, who does not drive but could walk to see her mother in a Norwood nursing home. "We loved that house—that home."

Past tense. Norwood's government, in a remarkably incestuous deal, accepted the developer's offer to pay the cost of the study that—surprise!—enabled the city to declare the neighborhood "blighted" and "deteriorating." NEWSWEEK reader, stroll around your neighborhood. Do you see any broken sidewalk pavement? Any standing water in a road? Any weeds? Such factors—never mind that sidewalks and roads are government's responsibility—were cited by the developer's study to justify Norwood's forcing the Gambles and their neighbors to sell to the developer so he could build condominiums, office buildings and stores.

Norwood's behavior is part of a national pattern: From 1998 through 2002, state and local governments seized or threatened to seize more than 10,000 homes, businesses, churches and pieces of land, not for "public use" but to enrich private interests, some of whose enhanced riches can be siphoned away by taxes. Such legalized theft—theft by government—does not use a gun, it just abuses the power of eminent domain. And it was declared constitutional by the U.S. Supreme Court in *Kelo v. New London* last year.

The Fifth Amendment includes this clause: ". . . nor shall private property be taken for public use, without just compensation." The Framers of the Bill of Rights did not scatter adjectives promiscuously: They said public use in order to restrict government to "takings" only for things directly owned by or primarily used by the general public, such as roads, bridges and public buildings. In 1954, the concept of "public use" was expanded to include curing urban blight. The *Kelo* case arose in New London, Conn., where the city government empowered a private entity to condemn property—a modest middle-class neighborhood—and give it to a private developer who would pay more taxes. The court ruled 5-4 in favor of New London.

Kelo demonstrated that anyone who owns a modest home or small business owns it only at the sufferance of a local government that might, on a whim of rapacity, seize it to enrich a more attractive potential taxpayer. But occasionally a Supreme Court decision disgusts and alarms so many people that there is a political recoil and broad social stirring. *Dred Scott v. Sanford* (1857) and *Roe v. Wade* (1973) were such decisions. The *Kelo* decision is proving to be the best thing that has happened since the New Deal to energize the movement to strengthen property rights.

The Gambles' plight—a quiet, blue-collar couple's life in ruins just as they are entering retirement—vividly illustrates what happens when property rights become too attenuated to protect the individual's zone of sovereignty against government power. Because such abuses are proliferating nationwide, people are pressuring state legislatures to forbid the seizure of property simply to give local governments—who never say they have enough revenues—the revenues they say they need. And Congress may forbid the use of federal funds for projects benefiting from such seizures. BB&T, the nation's ninth largest bank, has said it will not lend to developers who benefit from the power of eminent domain wielded to enrich them.

Reeling from the life-shattering effects of an uncircumscribed power of eminent domain, the Gambles are hoping for rescue by their state Supreme Court, before which they are represented by the Institute for Justice, a merry band of libertarian litigators. The Gambles have the dignified stoicism of uncomplicated people put upon by sophisticated people nimble with complex sophistries. Carl says, "We're paying a lot each month for storage" of their possessions that do not fit in his daughter's basement near the town of Independence, KY. Independence is what becomes tenuous when property rights become attenuated.

Appendix

The Origins of the American Bill of Rights

The U.S. Constitution as it was originally created and submitted to the colonies for ratification in 1787 did not include what we now call the Bill of Rights. This omission was the cause of much controversy as Americans debated whether to accept the new Constitution and the new federal government it created. One of the main concerns voiced by opponents of the document was that it lacked a detailed listing of guarantees of certain fundamental individual rights. These critics did not succeed in preventing the Constitution's ratification, but were in large part responsible for the existence of the Bill of Rights.

In 1787 the United States consisted of thirteen former British colonies that had been loosely bound since 1781 by the Articles of Confederation. Since declaring their independence from Great Britain in 1776, the former colonies had established their own colonial governments and constitutions, eight of which had bills of rights written into them. One of the most influential was Virginia's Declaration of Rights. Drafted largely by planter and legislator George Mason in 1776, the seventeen-point document combined philosophical declarations of natural rights with specific limitations on the powers of government. It served as a model for other state constitutions.

The sources for these declarations of rights included English law traditions dating back to the 1215 Magna Carta and the 1689 English Bill of Rights—two historic documents that provided specific legal guarantees of the "true, ancient, and indubitable rights and liberties of the people" of England. Other legal sources included the colonies' original charters, which declared that colonists should have the same "privileges, franchises, and immunities" that they would if they lived in England. The ideas concerning natural rights developed by John Locke and other English philosophers were also influential. Some of these concepts of rights had been cited in the Declaration of Independence to justify the American Revolution.

Unlike the state constitutions, the Articles of Confederation, which served as the national constitution from 1781 to 1788, lacked a bill of rights. Because the national government under the Articles of Confederation had little authority by design, most people believed it posed little threat to civil liberties, rendering a bill of rights unnecessary. However, many influential leaders criticized the very weakness of the national government for creating its own problems; it did not create an effective system for conducting a coherent foreign policy, settling disputes between states, printing money, and coping with internal unrest.

It was against this backdrop that American political leaders convened in Philadelphia in May 1787 with the stated intent to amend the Articles of Confederation. Four months later the Philadelphia Convention, going beyond its original mandate, created a whole new Constitution with a stronger national government. But while the new Constitution included a few provisions protecting certain civil liberties, it did not include any language similar to Virginia's Declaration of Rights. Mason, one of the delegates in Philadelphia, refused to sign the document. He listed his objections in an essay that began:

> There is no Declaration of Rights, and the Laws of the general government being paramount to the laws and constitution of the several States, the Declaration of Rights in the separate States are no security.

Mason's essay was one of hundreds of pamphlets and other writings produced as the colonists debated whether to ratify the new Constitution (nine of the thirteen colonies had to officially ratify the Constitution for it to go into effect). The supporters of the newly drafted Constitution became known as Federalists, while the loosely organized group of opponents were called Antifederalists. Antifederalists opposed the new Constitution for several reasons. They believed the presidency would create a monarchy, Congress would not be truly representative of the people, and state governments would be endangered. However, the argument that proved most effective was that the new document lacked a bill of rights and thereby threatened Americans with the loss of cherished individual liberties. Federalists realized that to gain the support of key states such as New York and Virginia, they needed to pledge to offer amendments to the Constitution that would be added immediately after its ratification. Indeed, it was not until this promise was made that the requisite number of colonies ratified the document. Massachusetts, Virginia, South Carolina, New Hampshire, and New York all included amendment recommendations as part of their decisions to ratify.

One of the leading Federalists, James Madison of Virginia, who was elected to the first Congress to convene under the new Constitution, took the lead in drafting the promised amendments. Under the process provided for in the Constitution, amendments needed to be passed by both the Senate and House of Representatives and then ratified by three-fourths of the states. Madison sifted through the suggestions provided by the states and drew upon the Virginia Declaration of Rights and other state documents in composing twelve amendments, which he introduced to Congress in September 1789. "If they are incorporated into the constitution," he argued in a speech introducing his proposed amendments,

> Independent tribunals of justice will consider themselves in a peculiar manner the guardians of those rights; they will be an impenetrable bulwark against every assumption of power

in the legislative or executive; they will be naturally led to resist every encroachment upon rights expressly stipulated for in the constitution by the declaration of rights.

After debate and some changes to Madison's original proposals, Congress approved the twelve amendments and sent them to the states for ratification. Two amendments were not ratified; the remaining ten became known as the Bill of Rights. Their ratification by the states was completed on December 15, 1791.

Supreme Court Cases Involving Property Rights

1833
Barron v. Baltimore

The Court stated that the Fifth Amendment's takings clause governed only federal government action, not actions of cities or states. It refused to require the state to pay just compensation to a wharf owner whose business was harmed by city development.

1897
Chicago, Burlington, and Quincey Railroad Company v. City of Chicago

The Court essentially overturned *Barron v. Baltimore* when it determined that the Fourteenth Amendment required the state to compensate a railroad for property seized in order to widen a street.

1922
Pennsylvania Coal Company v. Mahon

A coal company wanted to mine underneath a house, which would have caused the house to sink. A Pennsylvania law forbade mining under these circumstances. The Court found that the state's regulation was a taking because it effectively took away the company's coal.

1952
Youngstown Sheet and Tube Company v. Sawyer

The Court said that President Harry Truman could not seize the nation's steel mills in order to prevent a worker strike during the Korean War.

1978

Penn Central Transportation Company v. City of New York

In one of the earliest regulatory takings cases, the Court created a balancing test to determine whether a government regulation on private property was a taking. In this case, it ruled that declaring the facade of New York's Grand Central Station a historical landmark did not constitute a taking even though it prevented development of the property.

1980

Agins v. City of Tiburon

The Court declared that government regulation of private property is a taking if it does not substantially advance legitimate state interests.

1982

Loretto v. Teleprompter Manhattan CATV Corporation

A New York law said that landowners had to allow cable companies to install cable on properties, and landowners need only be paid one dollar for this access. The Court found that this permanent physical occupation of another's property was a taking.

1984

Hawaii Housing Authority v. Midkiff

A state law was passed to change the fact that a small number of people owned much of the privately held property in Hawaii. The Court found that the resulting takings, with just compensation, were rationally related to a conceivable public purpose.

1987

Nollan v. California Coastal Commission

In a case about exactions—a way to make a private landowner fund at least part of the costs of public improvements—the Court found that a required easement was a taking. The easement would have permitted the public to walk across an otherwise private beach in exchange for the private landowner being permitted to build a home on the property.

1992
Lucas v. South Carolina Coastal Council

Environmental regulations aimed at stopping beach erosion prevented a developer from building on two lots he had purchased before the area's beachfront management plan was implemented. The Court determined that the regulation was so excessive that it took all the value of the property away and was the equivalent of a physical appropriation.

1992
Yee v. City of Escondido

The Court declared that a rent-control ordinance did not result in a physical taking of property.

1994
Dolan v. City of Tigard

A storeowner was trying to expand her store and pave her parking lot. The Court found that the requirement that she dedicate part of her land to create a bicycle path was a taking.

1996
Bennis v. Michigan

A couple's jointly owned car was confiscated after the husband conducted illegal activity in it. The Court found no taking had occurred even though the wife was innocent and had no knowledge of the illegal activity taking place.

1997
Suitum v. Tahoe Regional Planning Agency

This case involved a procedural issue. The Court found that a property owner did not have to first try to sell developmental rights linked to a property in order to claim that a regulatory taking had occurred.

1999
Monterey v. Del Monte Dunes at Monterey, Ltd.

The Court permitted a jury trial to determine the amount of just compensation in a case where a developer was continuously denied the opportunity to build under any circumstances.

2001
Palazzolo v. Rhode Island

The Court examined state wetlands regulations that had foiled a developer's proposal to fill in wetlands and develop a beachfront recreational facility. The Court found that the mere fact that a landowner knew of the possibility of state regulation did not allow the state to take extreme or unreasonable regulatory measures.

2002
Tahoe-Sierra Preservation Council, Inc. v. Tahoe Regional Planning Agency

The Court examined a moratorium on development and found that a taking had not occurred.

2003
Brown v. Legal Foundation of Washington

This case examined state laws regarding interest on lawyers' trust accounts (money held on behalf of clients) and found that using such interest to fund legal services for the poor was not a taking.

2005
Lingle v. Chevron

The Court altered the result of its *Agins* decision and stated that regulatory takings challenges must be analyzed by looking at the burden placed on the property owner, not at the effectiveness of furthering a governmental interest.

2005

Kelo v. City of New London

The Court ruled that using eminent domain to take private property as part of an economic development plan is constitutional.

For Further Research

Books

Terry L. Anderson and Fred S. McChesney, *Property Rights: Cooperation, Conflict, and Law*. Princeton, NJ: Princeton University Press, 2002.

David Beito, Peter Gordon, and Alexander Tabarrok, eds., *The Voluntary City: Choice, Community, and Civil Society*. Ann Arbor: University of Michigan Press, 2002.

Jon W. Bruce and James W. Ely Jr., *Cases and Materials on Modern Property Law*. St. Paul: West, 2003.

Stephen Buckle, *Natural Law and the Theory of Property: Grotius to Hume*. New York: Oxford University Press, 1991.

Edwin S. Corwin, Harold W. Chase, and Craig R. Ducat, *The Constitution and What It Means Today*. Princeton, NJ: Princeton University Press, 1978.

James V. DeLong, *Property Matters: How Property Rights Are Under Assault and Why You Should Care*. New York: The Free Press, 1997.

James W. Ely Jr., ed., *Property Rights in American History*. New York: Garland, 1997.

Richard A. Epstein, *Takings: Private Property and the Power of Eminent Domain*. Cambridge, MA: Harvard University Press, 1985.

Doris and Harold Faber, *We the People: The Story of the United States Constitution Since 1787*. New York: Charles Scribner's Sons, 1987.

Eirik G. Furubotn and Svetozar Pejovich, eds., *The Economics of Property Rights*. Cambridge, MA: Ballinger, 1974.

Alfredo Garcia, *The Fifth Amendment: A Comprehensive Approach*. Westport, CT: Greenwood, 2002.

Steven Greenhut, *Abuse of Power: How the Government Misuses Eminent Domain*. Santa Ana, CA: Seven Locks, 2004.

Eugene W. Hickock Jr., ed., *The Bill of Rights: Original Meaning and Current Understanding*. Charlottesville: University Press of Virginia, 1990.

Milton R. Konvitz, *Bill of Rights Reader: Leading Constitutional Cases*. Ithaca, NY: Cornell University Press, 1973.

Leonard W. Levy, *Original Intent and the Framers' Constitution*. New York: Macmillan, 1988.

John Locke, *Second Treatise of Government (or An Essay Concerning Civil Government)*. New York: Cambridge University Press, 1988.

Richard Pipes, *Property and Freedom*. New York: Vintage, 2000.

Bernard H. Siegan, *Property and Freedom: The Constitution, the Courts, and Land-Use Regulation*. New Brunswick, NJ: Transaction, 1997.

Web Sites

FindLaw (www.findlaw.com). The site provides a search engine to assist with finding lawyers, court opinions, legal analysis, and other law-related materials.

The OYEZ Project: U.S. Supreme Court Multimedia (www.oyez.org). The project provides information about Supreme Court justices and summaries of important Supreme Court cases.

U.S. Supreme Court (www.supremecourtus.gov). The Court Web site provides basic information about the Supreme Court, cases on the current docket, prior opinions, and further materials for public information.

Index